THE SPANISH-AMERICAN WAR

Books by Albert Marrin

The Airman's War
Overlord
Victory in the Pacific
The Secret Armies
The Sea Rovers
War Clouds in the West
1812: The War Nobody Won
Aztecs and Spaniards
The Yanks Are Coming
Struggle for a Continent
The War for Independence
Inca and Spaniard
The Spanish-American War

THE SPANISH-AMERICAN WAR

ALBERT MARRIN

ATHENEUM
1991
NEW YORK
Collier Macmillan Canada
TORONTO
Maxwell Macmillan International Publishing Group
NEW YORK   OXFORD   SINGAPORE   SYDNEY

PHOTO CREDITS

National Archives: 2, 4, 8, 15, 36, 47, 67, 68, 71, 73, 79b, 91, 95, 97, 102, 109, 110, 115, 116, 118, 119, 120, 130, 138, 140, 142, 145, 156, 161
Library of Congress: 24, 79a, 85, 113, 126,
U.S. Navy: 121
New York Public Library: 87
The *Bee*, June 8, 1898: 19
New York *World*, Feb. 17, 1898: 29
McClures, Oct. 1898: 112
Century, May 1899: 124
The Life and Letters of Admiral Dewey: 55
The Splendid Little War: 57

Thanks to Valerie Jean Conner, Associate Professor, Department of History, Florida State University, for reading the manuscript.

Atheneum
Macmillan Publishing Company
866 Third Avenue
New York, NY 10022

Collier Macmillan Canada, Inc.
1200 Eglinton Avenue East
Suite 200
Don Mills, Ontario M3C 3N1

First Edition
Printed in the United States of America
1 2 3 4 5 6 7 8 9 10
Designed by Kimberly M. Hauck

Library of Congress Cataloging-in-Publication Data

Marrin, Albert.
The Spanish–American War/by Albert Marrin.—1st ed. p.   cm.
Includes bibliographical references (p.   ).
Summary: Describes the causes and events of the Spanish–American War and how it led to the involvement of the United States in the Philippine Insurrection.
ISBN 0-689-31663-1
1. United States—History—War of 1898—Juvenile literature.
[1. United States—History—War of 1898.] I. Title.
E715.M318 1991
973.8'9—dc20   *90-935 CIP AC*

This book is for Dr. Janice L. Gorn, our friend

"We're a gr-eat people," said Mr. Hennessey earnestly.
"We-ar-re," said Mr. Dooley. *"We ar-re that, an' the best iv it is,
we know we ar-re."*
—*Finley Peter Dunne,* Mr. Dooley in Peace and War, *1899*

Contents

⌷
Remember the Maine!

"When first in the dim light of early morning I saw the shores of Cuba rise and define themselves from the dark blue horizons, I felt as if I sailed with Captain Silver and first gazed on Treasure Island. Here was a place where real things were going on. . . . Here was a place where anything might happen. . . . Here I might leave my bones."
—*Winston S. Churchill,* My Early Life

The harbor, Havana, Cuba, Tuesday, February 15, 1898. It was a clear, starry night with the moon hanging overhead like an immense yellow globe. The air, heavy with the scent of tropical flowers, was warm, moist and sweet. So calm were the harbor waters that only an occasional ripple broke the reflection of the city lights.

The *Maine,* one of the first modern battleships built by the United States Navy, hung motionless on her anchor. Save for pinpoints of light shining through the portholes, her great bulk was shrouded in darkness. Officially, she was on a "goodwill" visit, but everyone knew there was another, unspoken, reason for her presence. There had recently been riots in the Cuban capital, and Washington wanted to show its readiness to protect American lives and property, by force if necessary. And a battleship could do that better than scores of diplomatic notes.

1

The **Maine** *sails proudly past the fortress guarding the entrance of the harbor of Havana, Cuba.*

Tonight, however, no one aboard the *Maine* was thinking of such serious matters. It had been a long day, and most crewmen were already in their hammocks on the berth deck in the forward part of the vessel. Some of the more energetic officers had gone ashore; it was carnival season in Havana and they didn't want to miss the fun. Most officers, however, were talking, reading, or just taking it easy in the wardroom near the aft (rear) gun turret. The men of the watch stood at their posts topside, bored by their assignment but glad not to be cooped up belowdecks.

Captain Charles D. Sigsbee sat at his desk, writing a letter to his wife. Although he loved her dearly, this wasn't a task he enjoyed doing. Months before, she'd given him a letter to mail to friends, which he'd put into a jacket pocket and forgotten about until tonight. He was trying to apologize when, at 9:30 P.M., Bugler Newton of the Marines sounded taps. *"Day is done, gone the sun. . . ."*

The Captain put down his pen to listen. That boy Newton, he thought. What a musician! He had a way with his instrument, a gift for closing the day on such a gentle, almost sad, note. As the last bars of the tune faded away, Sigsbee finished his letter, placed it in an envelope, and looked at his watch. It was exactly twenty minutes to ten.

Then it happened.

Suddenly a thundering explosion shook the *Maine* from end to end. This was followed by many smaller jolts as the ship's ammunition caught fire and exploded. The shells went off one after another, spraying red-hot splinters in every direction. Lights went out and clouds of black, suffocating smoke filled the spaces belowdecks. The vessel listed to port—titled to the left—and began to sink. Within seconds her dying noises became mingled with the sounds of dying men. There were whistling sounds as rushing water forced air through doors, hatches, and portholes. Steel plates groaned against one another, then snapped apart with earsplitting cracks.

"Oh, Jesus, Billy, I'm gone!" a sailor cried, clasping his hands over his burnt face.

"God help me! God help me!" another screamed as the water swept over him.

Captain Sigsbee groped his way through the blackness. Coming out on the main deck, he saw that nothing could be done to save the *Maine* and gave the order to abandon ship. While the undamaged lifeboats were being lowered, a Spanish cruiser sent its own lifeboats to haul the survivors from the water. Those Spanish sailors, brave men who knew their duty, risked their lives to help these strangers.

Daylight revealed the destructive scene. The *Maine* had

settled onto the harbor's muddy bottom, leaving only a mast and part of her upper deck exposed. Smoke still curled from the wreckage, and there was a strange gurgling sound: air bubbles escaping from flooded compartments. Captain Sigsbee, who'd returned to see things for himself, noticed that part of the berth deck was exposed. Later he reported: "On the white paint of the ceiling was the impression of two human bodies—mere dust." Of the 350 officers and men who'd sailed with him, 260 were killed by the explosion or drowned in the aftermath. Only 90 lived to tell the tale of that terrible night.

Spaniards, no less than Americans, were stunned by the disaster. The questions, like how the *Maine* exploded, or

A mass of twisted metal was all that was left of the **Maine** *after the explosion, the cause of which has never been fully explained.*

who was responsible and why, would come later. But now the Spanish authorities did whatever they could to comfort the victims. The wounded were sent to Spanish military hospitals and given the best care available. The dead were buried in a Havana cemetery with full Spanish military honors. During the days that followed, whenever a Spaniard met an American, he'd take off his hat, bow, and offer his regrets. Little did they know (then) that the explosion that sank the *Maine* would also signal the collapse of their empire and the rise of the United States to world power.

The Spanish empire would end where it began four centuries earlier—in Cuba. Located in the Caribbean Sea ninety miles south of Florida, the island was visited by Christopher Columbus during his first voyage in October 1492. After so many weeks at sea, it seemed like heaven to the weary explorer. "Everything is green," he wrote. "The singing of the birds is such that it seems as if one would never desire to depart. There are flocks of parrots that obscure the sun. There are trees of a thousand species, each having its peculiar fruit, and all of marvelous flavor."

The island's inhabitants were the Tainos, a gentle, peaceful folk who lived by farming and fishing. They called their home Colba, pronounced as Cuba by the Spaniards. They also had a habit that puzzled the newcomers. Columbus saw "many people who were going to their villages, both women and men, with a firebrand in the hand and herbs to drink the smoke thereof, as they are accustomed." Only later did he realize that he'd been the first European to see tobacco smokers. The natives

FLORIDA

Tampa

Gulf of
Mexico

Miami

Key West

Havana

CUBA

BAHAMAS

ATLANTIC

OCEAN

DOMINICAN
REPUBLIC

Santiago   HAITI

Siboney / Guantanamo
Daiquiri Bay

Caribbean Sea

PUERTO
RICO

San J

Ponce

JAMAICA

rolled the leaves ("herbs") into cigars—*tobacos* in their language. The Spaniards soon took up smoking and through them the habit spread to Europe. Early users smoked not only for pleasure, but because tobacco was supposed to cure various illnesses, among them cancer and lung diseases!

Cuba became one of the most important Spanish colonies in the New World. There, as elsewhere, the settlers turned out to be harsh masters. Claiming everything for themselves, they took the land and enslaved the natives, working them to exhaustion. Native beliefs were forbidden, their priests tortured, and the people forced to become Christians; those who kept their "false" beliefs were burnt alive or hacked to pieces. Landowners hunted escaped slaves with packs of fierce dogs. Entire villages were burnt to the ground and their inhabitants slaughtered for the landowners' "amusement." Within forty years of Columbus's landing, the Tainos had nearly vanished, creating a serious labor shortage for the Spanish rulers. It became necessary for them to send out expeditions to find other people to enslave. One of these expeditions was led by Hernán Cortés, who conquered the Aztec empire in Mexico. The Spaniards finally solved their labor problem by transporting enslaved Africans to Cuba.

By the mid-1800's, Cuba had a population of 1.6 million. Its rich soil made it the world's leading producer of sugar and one of the leading growers of tobacco and coffee. Although slavery had been abolished by then, there was still much dissatisfaction. Cubans, black and white, resented Spanish domination. Like the thirteen American colonies before them, they paid taxes to a foreign government over which they had no control. Spanish officials ruled the island in the interests of the mother country rather than the Cuban people. Spanish troops and police kept order. Spanish judges condemned those who protested, while Spanish firing squads executed them.

Resentment boiled over when the Cubans revolted in 1868. In that year two men stepped forward to lead the people in a war of independence. Máximo Gómez was a professional soldier with a talent for helping people work together. His friend, Antonio Maceo, was a descendant of African slaves. Known as the "Bronze Titan," Maceo was a skilled fighter said to have more lives than a cat; nothing scared him, and bullets seemed afraid of touching him.

The main street of a village on the outskirts of Santiago, Cuba. Under Spanish rule, most Cubans lived in poverty in villages of thatch-roofed huts without running water or proper sanitation.

Their war became a savage, bloody duel in which both sides were too weak to win and too strong to be defeated. As the war dragged on from year to year, Americans began to take notice of it. And what they saw concerned them. Some had investments in the island, which they might lose if fighting continued. Others saw the *insurrectos* (rebels) as freedom fighters, like the patriots who'd followed George Washington. Eager to help fellow patriots, they organized demonstrations against Spanish rule and collected money for the rebel cause. Often the money went into filibustering—the sending of men and weapons to aid rebels in foreign countries. Although filibustering was (and is) illegal, its supporters believed their cause was higher than any written law.

This belief led to the loss of the first American lives for

Cuban independence. In 1873, the steamer *Virginius* sailed from New York City with a cargo of guns for the rebels. Nearing the Cuban coast, she was taken by a Spanish cruiser; fifty-three of her crew, many of them Americans, were declared pirates and shot. Although the Spaniards later apologized for acting so "hastily," Americans never forgot, or forgave, the *Virginius* affair.

Spain finally ended the rebellion in 1878 through a combination of force and promises of reform. Thousands of Cubans, however, didn't trust Spanish promises and fled to the United States. There they settled in tightly knit communities, especially in New York City and Tampa, Florida, where they began small businesses. They also brought their skill at cigar-making, giving birth to a new American industry.

Their distrust of Spain was soon proven correct. Ending the war settled nothing. Once things became quiet, the Spaniards broke their promises and cracked down harder than ever. There were more arrests, more executions, more anger among the people. Cuba became a bomb waiting to explode.

José Martí lit the fuse. A small man with a drooping mustache, Martí was fifteen when the revolution began. Like many youngsters at the time, he supported independence with all his heart and soul. He was a gifted poet, whose poems glorified the rebels; he even started a newspaper to spread their ideas. The Spaniards promptly arrested him and sentenced him to hard labor in a stone quarry. After several months, he was sent to Spain and allowed to do as he pleased so long as he never returned to Cuba. He used his time to attend the University of Madrid and become a lawyer. Eventually he escaped and made his way to New York, where he joined a group of ex-rebels.

The revolution became Martí's whole life. Always on the move, he gave speeches and read his poems in every Cuban community he could reach. In his best-loved poem, he said:

With the poor of the earth
I wish to cast my lot.

Cuba, he insisted, was for all its children, rich and poor alike. He wanted to make it a prosperous, democratic republic where everyone might live in freedom and dignity. To prepare for the day of liberation, he founded the Cuban Revolutionary Party and a newspaper, *Patria (Fatherland)*. And because revolutions need weapons as well as ideas, he persuaded Cuban tobacco workers to donate one-tenth of their weekly wages for the purchase of guns and ammunition.

By the spring of 1895, the revolutionaries were ready. Agents were sent to Cuba to rouse the people and organize secret fighting units. In April, Martí, Gómez, and Maceo returned to their homeland. Although Martí died soon afterward in a skirmish with Spanish cavalry, the revolution swept across the island like a firestorm. Everywhere the people rallied to the cause of *Cuba libre!* Free Cuba!

Despite popular support, the rebels faced great odds. To begin with, they were outnumbered by better than five to one. At most there were 54,000 full-time *insurrectos,* compared to 240,000 Spanish soldiers. They had no uniforms, inadequate medical supplies, and little food. Their basic weapon was the machete, a knife two feet long, used to cut sugar cane and hack trails through the jungle. In battle the machete was a fearsome weapon, able to lop off an arm, or a head, with a single blow. Although there were some modern rifles, there were never enough. For the most part, rebels had old muskets, which might be as dangerous to the user as to his target; muskets were constantly blowing up in men's faces. Rebel cannons consisted of a few antiques that fired iron balls. One cannon, dating from the time of Columbus, was so rusty that it took weeks to clean and get into working order. It looked beautiful, and the rebels were proud of it. But as a weapon it was worthless, and blew up the first time it was fired at a Spanish fort. The Spaniards, however, had plenty of supplies, the latest repeating rifles, and artillery that fired explosive shells.

The rebels had no hope of defeating such an enemy in open battle. Rather than see his men slaughtered, Gómez, now the commander in chief, began guerrilla warfare. *Guerrilla* is Spanish for "little war," that is, war made by roving bands of fighters operating behind enemy lines. Cuba's "little war," however, was little only in name. The death and destruction it caused were enormous, scarring the land for a generation.

Insurrectos formed bands of one or two hundred under leaders chosen by themselves. Being small, these bands could hide easily, move swiftly, and strike without warning. Cuba, a land of rugged mountains, thick jungles and gloomy swamps, is ideal for this kind of warfare. Guerrillas could spring from nowhere, kill, and vanish like wisps of smoke. The idea was never to allow the Spaniard an advantage, avoiding strength and attacking weakness. When they outnumbered the regular troops, they'd go for the throat. When the troops outnumbered them, they'd run away. If guerrillas met unexpected resistance, they broke contact and fled to their hideouts until ready to strike elsewhere. Traveling lightly, they lived off gifts from friendly villagers and whatever they could take from the enemy. It was essential for the guerrillas to stay on good terms with the peasants, who provided valuable information and hid their wounded until they were able to travel. In fact, most guerrillas were peasants themselves.

No Spaniard was safe. Guerrillas might ambush a patrol here, raid an outpost there, or cause trouble anywhere. Individual soldiers were sniped at, clubbed, and slashed with machetes. Railroad track was torn up, telegraph lines cut, and bridges destroyed. Gómez's forces never tried to occupy a town for more than a few days. They'd overwhelm the garrison when they had it outnumbered, capture supplies, and then burn down the town to deprive the Spaniards of a base. The guerrillas then fled, leaving behind a small force to cover their escape. If the Spaniards followed, they were ambushed. These actions, though small in themselves, took place every day and were a constant drain on the Spaniards morale. Soldiers were always on edge, fearing every Cuban and not knowing when the next blow would fall or upon whom.

One enemy the Spaniards feared wasn't even human. Until the twentieth century, Cuba was the land of yellow fever, a deadly tropical disease. The native Cubans were largely resistant to the infection, unlike troops fresh from Europe. Yellow fever killed more Spaniards than rebel bullets. When asked to name his best commanders, Gómez replied, "Generals June, July, and August," the months when yellow fever was at its worst.

The guerrillas, however, did not rely on military action alone. Gómez realized that the Spaniards would try to hold Cuba as long as it remained valuable to them. He reasoned, then, that he'd make it worthless. During the summer of 1895, he began a scorched-earth campaign. "Blessed be the torch!" he shouted to his followers. He maintained that Cuba must be cleansed by fire, the old world destroyed to clear the way for the new. He ordered the sugar industry, the island's chief source of wealth, to be destroyed. All sugar plantations were to be burned. All workers were to leave their jobs in the sugar factories. Anyone who stayed on the job would be considered a traitor and shot. True, thousands of innocent workers would suffer, but that was a small price to pay for independence, he believed. He also believed that the people would blame the Spaniards, not his freedom fighters, for their misery—and he was right.

The Spaniards decided to fight fire with fire. In February 1896, a new military governor, General Valeriano Weyler, arrived in Cuba. Weyler is the most hated figure in Cuban history. Schoolchildren still recite a poem about him:

He has a face like a reptile, the
body of a dwarf,

The instinct of a jackal, the
soul of a dog.
Hypocrite! Coward! Vile
and obscene!

Weyler was no monster. A simple man with simple tastes, he ate little, slept on a straw mattress, and never smoked or drank hard liquor. He loved animals and would buy old horses to save them from the glue factory. Yet he was also a professional soldier with a job to do. It wasn't a pleasant job, or an easy one, but he felt soldiers must take their work as it comes. As a young man he'd served in Cuba and in campaigns against the warrior tribes of North Africa. During the American Civil War, he'd been Spain's official observer with the Union Army. General William Tecumseh Sherman became his idol— the same Sherman who said, "War is hell." In waging war, Sherman believed that maximum terror and destruction is, in the end, kinder to the enemy, since it forces him to surrender faster, thus saving lives. Sherman showed he meant business by cutting a swath of death and destruction across the Confederacy. Wherever he went, his troops terrorized the countryside, tearing up railroad tracks, looting plantations, and burning towns, leaving thousands of people homeless.

Weyler came to Cuba determined to put Sherman's tactics into practice. He began by limiting the guerrillas' freedom of movement. A belt two hundred yards wide was carved across the island from north to south. All trees

Spanish "justice" was swift and ruthless. These men are about to be shot by firing squad at Santiago. Notice the pockmarked wall, indicating that many others had been executed on this spot in the past.

within the belt were cut down and formed into a barrier on either side. Between them was a military railroad with armored cars bristling with guns. Forts with watchtowers were built every quarter-mile and defended by cannon and barbed wire entanglements; Weyler was the first to use barbed wire in warfare on a large scale. Rebels seldom attacked the belt head on, and when they did they suffered. Among those killed was none other than Antonio Maceo, Gómez's second in command. At last, the "Bronze Titan" met a bullet that wasn't "afraid" of him.

Weyler's next move was against the very heart of guerrilla power. The governor decided that since the peasants helped the enemy most, they must be removed from the countryside. So began the "reconcentration" system, one of the cruelest forms of warfare ever devised. Peasants were herded into certain towns or camps set up in the open and guarded by Spanish troops. If they came peacefully, they were promised housing, food, and work. If they resisted, or if they were found outside their proper area, they were shot.

Despite Weyler's promises, the *reconcentrados* lived under a sentence of death. Forced to live in abandoned warehouses without beds, toilet facilities, or medical attention, they fell ill and died in droves. Food was scarce, and their only "work" was scrounging in the garbage pails outside Spanish army kitchens. Sick, shrunken people wandered about, living ghosts waiting for the end. Children with running sores and bloated bellies threaded their way around bodies lying in the roads.

To keep the peasants where they belonged, Weyler had his soldiers turn the countryside into a desert. Army patrols burned crops, killed farm animals, poisoned wells, and destroyed buildings. William J. Calhoun, an American government official, described the scene during a fifty-mile journey:

I travelled by rail from Havana to Matanzas. The country outside of the military posts was practically depopulated. Every house had been burned, banana trees cut down, cane fields swept with fire, and everything in the shape of food destroyed. It was as fair a landscape as mortal eye ever looked upon; but I did not see a house, man, woman or child, horse, mule, or cow, nor even a dog. I did not see a sign of life, except an occasional vulture or buzzard sailing through the air. The country was wrapped in the stillness of death and the silence of desolation.

As near as we can tell, one-quarter of the Cuban population—400,000 men, women, and children—died because of Weyler's scheme.

For them, war truly was hell.

Americans looked toward Cuba with growing concern. The United States is a nation of immigrants. During the 1890s, millions came to its shores seeking a better life. Often these people—Poles, Italians, Russians, Irish, Germans, and others—were refugees from oppression in Europe. They knew the meaning of military rule, secret police, and fake trials. "Freedom" and "independence" were not merely words to them. They were real things, worthy things, and anyone willing to fight for them automatically had their sympathy.

The Cubans made sure that Americans saw their cause in its "true" light. Before Martí left for the invasion, he had set up a junta—council—of Cuban patriots and

American sympathizers. The junta's task was to supply American newspapers, especially those in New York City, with propaganda disguised as news stories. Once a week, sometimes more often, it told reporters of the latest Spanish crimes and Cuban victories. This was a useful tactic, for it, more than anything, swayed American public opinion.

These stories also played into the hands of the "yellow press." During the past fifteen years, a new type of newspaper had come into existence in New York, the journalistic capital of the United States. The old-style newspaper had been written for the educated reader. Dull and relatively expensive, it was printed in small type and had no illustrations. Its purpose was not to get its readers excited, much less angry, but to present the facts and let readers judge for themselves. This was a good policy, but it sold few papers and made little profit for newspaper owners.

Things began to change when Joseph Pulitzer took over the *New York World*. Pulitzer, who'd arrived in the United States as a poor immigrant from Hungary, wanted his paper to reach everyone, not just the upper classes. The *World* was redesigned to attract the general public. Beginning in 1883, it featured rip-roaring accounts of murders, suicides, scandals, and disasters. These were given in banner headlines, simple words, short paragraphs, and eye-catching drawings. Sports pages, columns on personal grooming, and crossword puzzles were added. The *World* even appealed to the kiddies with color comic strips. Its most popular comic-strip character was the Yellow Kid, a tiny terror in a bright yellow nightshirt. Pulitzer was so successful that other papers quickly copied his methods. Each featured sensational stories and had a comic charac-

A rival newspaper pokes fun at William Randolph Hearst, portraying him as the real-life Yellow Kid.

ter like the Yellow Kid—hence the phrase "yellow press."

Pulitzer's greatest admirer was William Randolph Hearst. The son of a Colorado silver prospector who'd struck it rich, Hearst used daddy's money to buy the failing *New York Journal.* "Willie"—a nickname he despised—proved to be a shrewd businessman. He increased the paper's size, sold copies for a penny, and gave the public a steady diet of articles like "Why Young Girls Kill Themselves" and "Strange Things Women Do for Love." Unfortunately, New York wasn't big enough for two newspaper tycoons. By 1895 the *World* and the *Journal* were locked in a bitter struggle for survival. Each tried to attract the other's readers with spicier stories, bigger contests, and more valuable prizes. And, of course, each used Cuba as ammunition in their circulation war.

The junta's news releases were taken at face value. Gómez's guerrillas, as we've seen, had no qualms about shooting workers and destroying private property in order to further their cause. But they were "freedom fighters," and so their outrages weren't reported by the yellow press, which found it more sensational—and profitable—to focus on the atrocities of "Butcher Weyler." The result of such one-sidedness was to inflame American public opinion. Slowly, noisily, the yellow press was setting the stage for a wider conflict.

Hearst, however, was the chief offender. The press, he declared, was the people's true representative. He wrote in a *Journal* article:

> *The force of the newspaper is the greatest force in civilization.*
>
> *Under republican government, newspapers form and express public opinion.*
>
> *They suggest and control legislation.*
>
> *They declare wars.*
>
> *They punish criminals. . . .*
>
> *Newspapers control the nation because they represent the people.*

They declare wars! They control the nation! No doubt about it: Willie Hearst was a dangerous fellow. Although no one had elected him to any office, he believed it his right to push the nation into war. In the name of "justice" for Cuba and profits for himself, he worked tirelessly for a Spanish-American war.

Nothing would keep Hearst from a juicy story, not even the truth. If there wasn't enough exciting news to write about, he made up his own. He was so bent upon war that, in 1897, he sent the artist Frederic Remington to Havana to cover it when it began. When Remington reported that Havana was quiet and that he wanted to go home, Hearst wired: "Please remain. You furnish the pictures, and I'll furnish the war."

These were not idle words. A few weeks later, Hearst printed a story about three Cuban women expelled by Weyler for aiding the rebels. When they boarded an American ship at Havana, Spaniards hustled them into a cabin and put them through a strip search to see if they were carrying secret messages. A large drawing showed bearded detectives staring at a young, and very naked, woman. "Does Our Flag Shield Women?" the *Journal* asked in screaming headlines. "Refined Young Woman Stripped And Searched By Brutal Spaniards While Under Our Flag."

The article was deliberately misleading. The women had indeed aided the rebels. They had been stripped, not by men, but by women police officers. Meantime, the misrepresentation was lost in a swirl of other, more sensational, stories. Hearst laughed all the way to the bank; that issue of the *Journal* sold nearly a million copies, until then the largest newspaper run in history.

The more Americans heard of "Poor Little Cuba" and "Butcher Weyler," the angrier they became. Protest meetings and demonstrations were held in New York, Chicago, and other major cities. Voters signed petitions to their congressmen and state legislators demanding intervention on behalf of the rebels. Youngsters collected money to aid the rebels and discussed Weyler's crimes during current events time in school.

Other Americans felt that words weren't enough; they demanded action and were ready to put their own lives on the line. No fewer than three thousand men volunteered to fight alongside Gómez's guerrillas; at one point the junta announced that it had more recruits than it could handle. The junta's announcement, however, had little effect. Men continued to enlist, among them fifty-five Texas cowboys and a company of Texas Rangers. Frederick Funston, whom we'll meet later, became commander of the rebel artillery. Many recruits took basic training at a rebel-run camp near Boston.

Scores of filibusters sailed for Cuba from Atlantic and Gulf Coast ports. The most daring of these was "Dynamite Johnny" O'Brien, a colorful character who specialized in smuggling explosives. O'Brien feared nobody, not even Butcher Weyler. During one expedition, he slipped into Havana and left his calling card at the general's palace. Weyler was not amused. He hired private detectives to spy on O'Brien, but all they could show for their efforts were burns and bruises. Whenever Mrs. O'Brien saw suspicious men lurking near their house, she'd let go with pots of boiling water.

The mounting hatred of Spain had no effect on President Grover Cleveland. Stories in the yellow press, he growled, were nonsense, the fantasies of blowhards, windbags, and warmongers. Both sides in Cuba were guilty of atrocities, he said. A plague on both their houses! As President his duty was clear: to keep his country peaceful and prosperous, without meddling in other people's quarrels. Congressional pleas for a "stronger" policy toward Spain were ignored by the White House. Cleveland even ordered the Coast Guard to stop the filibustering. It tried, but, like drug smuggling today, the problem kept growing. Even so, when he left office in 1897, Cleveland could point with pride to the fact that America was at peace with the world.

Cleveland handed over the Cuban problem to his successor, William McKinley. Like Cleveland, President McKinley hated war. As an eighteen-year-old volunteer, he'd joined the Union Army in the early days of the Civil War. He knew the horrors of war firsthand, having fought in three major battles, including Antietam, which was that war's single bloodiest day. Those battlefield experiences scarred his memory for life. "I have been through one war," he told a friend years later. "I have seen the dead piled up, and I do not want to see another." But if the Spaniards thought the President was soft, they didn't know their man. Although he hated war, he'd never accept peace at any price. He'd try to keep the peace, so long as it was with honor and justice.

In September 1897, McKinley began to put pressure on the Spanish government in Madrid. Cuba, he said, was a bloody mess with no end in sight. America's patience was limited; it would not tolerate Weyler's atrocities. Unless things changed soon, public opinion would force him to

take drastic action. The words "drastic action" were carefully chosen, for statesmen used them as a polite term for war.

This was a challenge the Spaniards could not ignore. Spain at this time was no longer a world power. Once she'd held the largest empire in history, larger even than that of ancient Rome. But after centuries of abuse, her South American colonies and Mexico had broken away in the 1820s, leaving her only Cuba and Puerto Rico in the New World and the Philippine Islands in the Pacific. Having little industry or foreign trade, but much poverty and superstition, Spain was in many ways still living in the Middle Ages. If she hoped to keep the crumbs of her empire, she had to avoid a war

President William McKinley in his White House office. A man of peace, McKinley failed in his efforts to avoid war with Spain.

she couldn't afford and had little hope of winning. For a time it seemed that McKinley's methods were working. The Spanish government removed Weyler and promised to end his reconcentration policy. It even gave the Cubans a share in running their country. These concessions, however, satisfied no one. Gómez's rebels, encouraged by the hope of American intervention, demanded full independence. The Spaniards in Cuba, fearing that Madrid had gone too far, took to the streets in protest. In January 1898 some of Weyler's troops joined them. The mood turned ugly, then violent. Foreigners were roughed up by angry crowds. Foreign-owned shops were looted. Worse, there were rumors of a plot to murder all foreigners, particularly Americans.

McKinley lost no time in ordering the *Maine* to Havana. His meaning was clear: If the Spaniards couldn't (or wouldn't) protect American lives and property, they'd have to answer to the ship's big guns. Although the yellow press cheered the President's action, others thought he was playing with fire. Ohio Senator Mark Hanna compared it to "waving a match in an oil well for fun."

Things seemed to quiet down after the *Maine*'s arrival on January 15, but that was just the calm before the storm. Early the next month, Dupuy de Lôme, Spanish ambassador to the United States, wrote a letter to a friend in Cuba. In it he described McKinley as a "hack politician," a weak, foolish man who only wanted people to like him.

De Lôme's letter didn't remain private for long. A Cuban spy opened it, photographed it, and sent the copy to Willie Hearst. Hearst's *Journal* unfurled a banner headline: "Worst Insult to the United States in History!" People shouted for the ambassador's blood, but he resigned before things became nasty.

Meantime, the *Maine* rode at anchor in Havana harbor. Since she was on a "goodwill" visit, sailors were given shore leave. They were on their best behavior, and local shopkeeps did a good trade in souvenirs, cigars, and rum. Townspeople came to the waterfront to admire the great white ship glistening in the sunlight. Yet there were also those who glowered at *los Américanos* and spat behind their backs when they walked by.

One day Captain Sigsbee and his officers attended a bullfight. His hosts were polite but cold. Throughout the bullfight, Spaniards pointed at them as they spoke among themselves. After the show, as Sigsbee stood up to leave, someone thrust a circular printed in Spanish into his hand. In large letters across the top it said: "Spaniards! Long Live Spain With Honor!" This was followed by an attack on "these Yankee pigs" who'd come to Havana in their "rotten" ship. It ended with a call to arms: "Death to Americans!" Just to make sure Sigsbee got the message, there was scribbled in English at the bottom: "Look out for your ship!"

The Captain did just that. In the days that followed, he put the *Maine* on full battle alert. The night watch was doubled and shells stacked near the guns. Steam was kept up in the boilers so that the gun turrets could be turned toward the city immediately. Sigsbee wasn't taking any chances—except one he couldn't imagine.

During the evening of February 15, his ship blew up and sank. Far away, in Washington, D.C., President McKinley had gone to bed early. Shortly after 2 A.M., a watchman woke him to answer the telephone. Secretary of the Navy John Long came on the line with the news. McKinley stood there in his pajamas, holding the receiver with a trembling hand. "The *Maine* blown up!" he muttered, hardly able to believe his ears. "The *Maine* blown up!" Then he dressed and called an emergency meeting of the cabinet.

Meantime, telegraph wires were humming in newspaper offices across the country. About an hour after the President awoke, the telephone on Willie Hearst's night table rang. It was a call from the *Journal* newsroom. The night editor had called to report the sinking and that he'd put the story on page one, along with other big stories. Hearst was overjoyed. There are no other big stories, he shouted. The *Maine* must take up the entire front page. "This means war!"

The *Journal's* first edition hit the streets with a slogan that would soon sweep the country:

> *Remember the* Maine*!*
> *To hell with Spain!*

And the only way to remember the tragedy was with Spanish blood.

Such a demand would have been impossible twenty-five years earlier. At that time, the Civil War had been over only eight years.* Memories of the struggle were still vivid, and only lunatics dreamed of repeating such an ordeal. But as time passed, memories of its horrors faded. Veterans, eager to recapture their youth, looked back on it as an adventure filled with romance and glory. Young

*The Civil War lasted from 1861 to 1865.

men, raised on heroic war stories, longed for adventures of their own. The new spirit was captured in snappy marches like John Philip Sousa's "Stars and Stripes Forever" and in "There'll Be A Hot Time in the Old Town Tonight," the most popular song of the nineties.

President McKinley was in no hurry to go to war. Before taking that terrible step, he wanted to be sure that there was really something to fight about. There were questions to be answered. How did the *Maine* sink? Was the explosion inside the vessel or outside? If inside, it was the result of an accident. If outside, it had to be due to a mine. If it was a mine, who planted it and why?

A naval board of inquiry was ordered to study the wreck and give its findings as soon as possible. The board, headed by Rear Admiral William T. Sampson, commander of the Atlantic Fleet, went to work immediately. Survivors were interviewed. Hundreds of photographs were taken and studied. Divers were sent to discover whatever they could. Since they'd noticed that some of the ship's armor plates were bent inward, the board blamed the sinking on a mine explosion outside the forward magazine, the room where ammunition for the ship's big guns was stored. It added that there was no evidence as to who'd set off the mine.

The Spaniards also held a board of inquiry, which came to the opposite conclusion. Everything, it noted, pointed to an inside explosion, the result of some unknown cause. The reasons given were logical and based upon what eyewitnesses *didn't* see. No one, for example, had seen a geyser, a sure sign of an underwater blast. There were no dead fish in the water, and nobody had felt a shock wave, which a mine would have caused. Even if a mine had sunk

Department of ...

863,956 **The** **World.** 863,956

WORLDS CIRCULATED YESTERDAY "Circulation Books Open to All." "Circulation Books Open to All." WORLDS CIRCULATED YESTERDAY

VOL. XXXVIII. NO. 13,398. NEW YORK, THURSDAY, FEBRUARY 17, 1898. PRICE

MAINE EXPLOSION CAUSED BY BOMB OR TORPEDO?

Capt. Sigsbee and Consul-General Lee Are in Doubt---The World Has Sent a Special Tug, With Submarine Divers, to Havana to Find Out---Lee Asks for an Immediate Court of Inquiry---Capt. Sigsbee's Suspicions.

CAPT. SIGSBEE, IN A SUPPRESSED DESPATCH TO THE STATE DEPARTMENT, SAYS THE ACCIDENT WAS MADE POSSIBLE BY AN ENEMY.

Dr. E. C. Pendleton, Just Arrived from Havana, Says He Overheard Talk There of a Plot to Blow Up the Ship---Capt. Zalinski, the Dynamite Expert, and Other Experts Report to The World that the Wreck Was Not Accidental---Washington Officials Ready for Vigorous Action if Spanish Responsibility Can Be Shown---Divers to Be Sent Down to Make Careful Examinations.

The sinking of the Maine *sent a thrill of horror across the United States. This artist's representation appeared on the front page of the* New York World *the day after the disaster.*

the *Maine,* Spain had no reason for planting it. Spain had nothing to gain and everything to lose by sinking the *Maine.* Surely, that would bring war with the United States, the very thing she'd been trying to avoid. If anyone had an interest in starting a war, it was the Cuban rebels, who knew that they had no chance of winning without American intervention. But they had neither the skill nor the resources to make and explode the type of mine needed to sink a battleship.

Neither report proved its case beyond the shadow of a doubt. In 1976, Admiral Hyman G. Rickover, "the father of the nuclear navy," wrote *How the Battleship "Maine" Was Destroyed*. After examining all available information and comparing it with the latest scientific findings, he concluded that the sinking was accidental.

The most likely cause, said Rickover, was spontaneous combustion—something bursting into flame by itself, without heat from an outside source. Warships at that time had their coal bunkers—storage rooms—built around their magazines, where ammunition is stored, and engine rooms for added protection against enemy shells. A smoldering coal fire in a sealed bunker could have heated the steel plates separating it from the magazine to the point where one of the shells exploded, setting off a chain reaction. Rickover admitted, however, that he couldn't prove this, either. It was only the most likely cause. The mystery of the *Maine* remains unsolved. It probably never will be solved, for she was eventually raised from Havana harbor, towed out to sea, and sunk in deep water.

The American public wasn't interested in the fine points of naval engineering. Despite the caution of its own board of inquiry, it "knew" that Spain had sunk the *Maine*. The yellow press had said so, explaining how the deed was done with drawings by artists who'd never been to Havana or seen a naval mine. People needed no further explanations and wanted no apologies. Spanish flags were burned by crowds demanding vengeance. Even Congressmen, who should have known better, began to beat the war drums.

President McKinley, still hoping for a peaceful solution, became the target of public abuse. Mobs burned him in effigy. His picture was hissed in theaters. Visitors to the Senate and House galleries sat wrapped in American flags, howling for war. Politicians used language that made the de Lôme letter sound like a Sunday school lesson. The President was accused of being weak, ignorant, cowardly. "Wobbly Willie," Congressmen called him. He was "a white-livered cur," said a Navy Department official named Theodore Roosevelt. "The President," Roosevelt continued, "has no more backbone than a chocolate eclair." Things reached the point where members of the House of Representatives burst out in choruses of "Dixie" and "The Battle Hymn of the Republic," songs popular during the Civil War. Members gathered in the House lobby to sing, "We'll Hang General Weyler to a Sour Apple Tree."

These taunts took their toll on the President. McKinley became nervous; he'd pace for hours, hands clenched behind his back, wearing a path through the White House grounds. Worry lines appeared on his face, bags formed under his eyes. He needed sedatives in order to sleep. An old friend recalled how he "broke down and cried like a boy of thirteen."

At last the President decided that he must follow the crowd. On April 11 he asked Congress for authority to use force to end the troubles in Cuba. Eight days later Congress declared Cuba independent, demanded that Spain leave the island, and asked the President to take military action if she refused. On April 25 Congress formally declared war.

Victory at Sea

"Didn't Admiral Dewey do wonderfully well? I got him the position out there in Asia last year, and I had to beg hard to do it; and the reason I gave was that we might have to send him to Manila. And we sent him—and he went!"
—Theodore Roosevelt to a friend, May 3, 1898

The Spanish-American War was the most popular of all our wars. When it began, people welcomed it as a national holiday. Crowds cheered as bands played patriotic tunes. There were parades galore, and Old Glory never flew more proudly. Patriots—everyone claimed to be a patriot then—honored the flag each in his own way. They flew it from the windows of city tenements and the roofs of country mansions. Schoolchildren wore it on celluloid buttons. Bicyclists strung striped bunting through the spokes of their wheels. In Washington, a young woman paraded in an outfit resembling a soldier's uniform. Upon opening the coat, she revealed a silk blouse of red, white, and blue stripes. Her eyes, a reporter noted, shone as brightly as the stars on the flag.

Americans looked forward to a quick, easy campaign against the "garlics," their nickname for Spaniards. They expected to call up the army, invade Cuba, and set it free without half-trying. Yet the first victory came in a way few expected. It came, not on land in Cuba, but at sea on the other side of the globe. On May 1, 1898, Commodore George Dewey sank the enemy's Pacific Fleet at Manila Bay in the Philippine Islands. It was a miracle—to land-lubbers. But for navy men it came as no surprise. It was their reward for years of effort and, they hoped, it pointed to the future. To understand how it came about, we must first understand the growth of United States seapower.

During the Civil War, the Union had built a magnificent navy. Numbering 626 vessels, it was not only the world's largest but the most up-to-date. Had John Paul Jones, the naval hero of the American Revolution, returned in 1865, he would have rubbed his eyes in disbelief. The finest ships were no longer made of wood and powered by sails, but were ironclad monsters driven by steam engines. Nor were their guns the familiar smooth-bores that fired solid iron cannonballs. They were "rifles," so-called because they had riflings, grooves cut inside the barrel to make an explosive shell spin in the same way a quarterback throws a football; spinning gives both shells and footballs speed, accuracy, and distance. These guns were also mounted in revolving turrets able to turn in any direction.

With the coming of peace, Americans abandoned their navy. This was done not out of anger or ignorance, but because it made good sense. Navies were for fighting on the high seas, far from our shores. But America had no foreign enemies. After the Civil War, the nation turned inward, to build cities and factories, to tame a continent and bind it together with railroads. Its "useless" warships were sold at bargain prices, broken up for scrap, or allowed to rust at dockside. By 1881, the United States ranked below Chile and China as a seapower. Of its twenty-six ships, all but four were wooden hulks, old floating coffins that could easily be blasted to splinters.

But by then things had begun to change. The frontier, the magnet that had pulled Americans westward for two centuries, was closing. There were no more giveaways of government land. Fewer people were earning their living by farming and ranching. Trade with the outside world was growing in importance, and with it the importance of the sea. Once again the United States needed a powerful navy.

That navy owed much to Captain (later Admiral) Alfred Thayer Mahan and his followers. A professor in the United States Naval Academy at Annapolis, Maryland, Mahan was a scholar rather than a fighting sailor. While at the academy, he wrote a book entitled *The Influence of Seapower upon History*. In it he quoted the English explorer Sir Walter Raleigh: "Whosoever commands the oceans of the world, commands the trade of the world. And whosoever commands the trade of the world, commands the riches of the world and consequently the world itself."

History's most important lesson, Mahan noted, was that seapower decided the fate of nations and empires. Without command of the sea, no people had ever remained great or prosperous. America would soon produce more goods than she'd be able to use at home. When that time came, she'd have to sell the surplus overseas or lose out to foreign competitors. In order to hold her own, she needed three things. The first was a battle fleet able to protect her merchant ships and coastal cities. Second, she needed overseas bases for repairing and refueling her warships. Finally, because she had two coastlines to defend, she must build a canal across Central America to shorten the distance between her Atlantic and Pacific coasts. Although Mahan thought the canal should go through Nicaragua, it was cut across the isthmus of Panama a few years later.

Mahan's ideas gained influence on both sides of the Atlantic. In the early 1890s, Great Britain and Germany, Europe's leading industrial nations, began to upgrade their fleets. Congress also began voting money for warships. This "new navy," as it was known, had the deadliest war machines ever built in America. Manned by well-trained crews, they could hold their own against anything that floated.

The basic warship types were the cruiser and destroyer, swift vessels armed with medium-sized guns and torpedoes, meant to attack enemy merchantmen and protect their own battleships. Compared to the battleship, however, they were like kittens against tigers.

Battleships were known as "capital ships," that is, the most important vessels in the fleet. The *Maine* and the *Texas,* America's first modern battleships, were launched in 1890. Smaller than later models, they were known as "second-class" battleships. They were quickly followed by the "first-class" *Oregon* (1893), *Indiana* (1895), *Massachusetts* (1896), and *Iowa* (1897). As their names indicate, American battleships were always named after states.

The science of building warships progressed by leaps and bounds after the Civil War. At the turn of the century, the average battleship cost $3 million and took from

The Oregon *was America's newest and fastest battleship during the struggle with Spain.*

two to three years to build. By today's standards, they were cheap; our B-2 Stealth bombers cost $532 million *each*. Yet at a time when workers earned fifty cents a day, $3 million was a fantastic sum of money.

Big! is the only word for a battleship. A first-class vessel of that time measured 350 feet long by 70 feet wide and weighed about eleven thousand tons. An average of five hundred officers and men were needed to handle it on the high seas. Powered by steam engines, its boilers gobbled up enormous amounts of coal. If placed end to end, the boilers would form a tunnel 156 feet long, large enough for a small railroad train to pass through. At a top speed of sixteen knots (roughly eighteen miles an hour), they burned ten tons of coal an hour. Coal was known as "black diamonds," and it was the key to seapower. Without it, a fleet was as helpless as a school of beached whales.

Those responsible for a vessel's coal were the "black

gang," so-called because black dust covered them from head to toe. The dust got into their pores, turning their skin a deep purple that could never be washed away. The black gang was made up of various specialists. Coal passers hauled it aboard in heavy sacks, which were dumped into little carts and emptied down chutes into the bunkers. Trimmers then leveled it and packed it tightly into place. Stokers, who had the nastiest job of all, shoveled it into the boilers. Naked except for underpants and shoes, their bodies glistening with sweat, they worked in temperatures of 170° Fahrenheit and more. They worked steadily, pausing only to douse their heads in the tubs of water placed on the floor near each boiler. Even so, men fainted from the heat and had to be taken topside. The fresh air worked wonders, and they usually recovered within minutes.

Most of a battleship's weight was made up of armor plate. A belt of steel eighteen inches thick ran along the waterline. This was backed by six inches of wood, another two inches of steel plates and the coal bunkers, which gave another ten feet of protection. The pointed bow was specially reinforced, forming a battering ram that could smash through the sides of most vessels.

The battleship's main weapons, however, were its rifles. United States battleships carried four thirteen-inch rifles mounted in two armored turrets. The size of a gun is measured not by the length of its barrel but by the width of the shell it fires, which means that a thirteen-inch rifle took a shell thirteen inches wide. Shells came in two separate parts: an eleven-hundred-pound explosive warhead and a 520-pound bag of gunpowder to send it on its way. When the warhead left the barrel, it traveled at a speed of twenty-one hundred feet per second and could reach a target ten miles away. Each rifle was forty feet long and weighed 60.5 tons. In addition, a battleship had eight eight-inch and four six-inch guns. It also had two masts, but these no longer carried sails. Masts now served as observation posts and had small, quick-firing guns called "lead squirters" mounted at the top.*

Navy men were all volunteers. Ordinary sailors, nicknamed "bluejackets," often enlisted as teenagers; the minimum age was seventeen, although big lads as young as fourteen managed to sneak past the recruiters. In order to be accepted, you had to be healthy and able to read; a high school diploma was not required. Officers were graduates of the Naval Academy and had studied naval engineering, gunnery, and navigation. Pay depended on one's education and responsibilities. A bluejacket made twenty-four dollars a month; an ensign, or junior officer, earned one hundred dollars a month; a rear admiral, then the highest rank in the service, received five hundred dollars a month.

The bluejacket's daily needs were taken care of by Uncle Sam. These had to be few and simple, since fuel and equipment claimed most space aboard a warship. Although officers lived in tiny cabins, crewmen were crowded into the few open spaces belowdecks. Each man's gear consisted of two winter and three summer uniforms, shoes, socks, underwear, mess kit, and a

*Battleships constantly increased in size and hitting power. Forty years later, during World War II, American battleships weighed forty-five thousand tons, cruised at thirty-three knots, had twenty-five-hundred-man crews, and carried nine sixteen-inch rifles. Some Japanese battleships mounted nineteen-inch rifles that could throw a one-ton warhead twenty-two miles. Today's battleships, refitted World War II vessels, also carry Tomahawk cruise missiles tipped with nuclear warheads.

wooden "ditty box" for personal things. Water was scarce, so he received one bucket a day for drinking and washing himself and his clothes. Since there was no refrigeration, he seldom saw fresh food while at sea. If it couldn't be dried or pickled, it didn't go aboard. Thus his diet consisted mainly of beans, rice, salt pork, "canned Willie" (corned beef), and hardtack, which were square, flat loaves of bread baked hard as dog biscuits. Yet skilled cooks could turn the plainest things into tasty dishes. They might serve plum duff, a pudding made from a paste of flour, water, and raisins. Then there was burgoo, a mixture of molasses and broken hardtack. Slush, slum, and rope-yarn were stews that tasted better than their names sounded. Everything was washed down with java—mugs of steaming black coffee.

Bluejackets liked to say that they were the only people who ate under where they slept and slept under where they ate. This was no riddle but the plain truth. Eating was done on wooden tables and benches stored between the overhead deck beams and lowered by ropes when needed; the meal over, they were cleaned and hoisted back into place. Sleeping was in hammocks slung from hooks driven into those same beams. Each morning hammocks were folded, tied, and stored in compartments topside. The hammock, incidentally, was a New World invention; Columbus's men borrowed it from the native peoples of the Caribbean during his first voyage.

A thousand-and-one things needed to be done to keep a vessel shipshape. Engineers tended the engines like their own children. Armorers saw to the guns and ammunition. Deckhands were always holystoning, scrubbing the wooden decks with coarse sandstone bricks. Cobblers and tailors practiced their trades. Since rust is the enemy of steel, work crews constantly polished and painted metalwork. Drills were held for taking battle stations, handling weapons, firefighting, damage control, abandoning ship, and launching lifeboats.

Evenings were normally the slow time at sea, a time for relaxation. In the hour or two before taps, sailors amused themselves with card games and "Spanish pool," a form of checkers. Men joked and told of past voyages. They sang, played accordions, and danced with each other, taking turns at the men's and women's parts. Old-timers, fellows with shaggy beards and leathery faces, still clung to ancient superstitions. One was that if a sailor died at sea, his soul lived on in the body of a white sea gull. Nearly all warships had mascots, for wherever they went there was always a stray cat or dog, monkey or parrot, which someone took a liking to. Vessels that took pigs as their official mascots always named them "Dennis."

Every bluejacket looked forward to "liberty." When his ship reached port, those with no demerits against their name were allowed to go ashore. Sailors on liberty saw the sights, shopped, and collected souvenirs. Some collected works of art—on their own skin. They visited tattoo parlors, where, for a few dollars, they could be decorated with their own initials or a huge heart with their girl's name in red letters. One fellow had a fat "boa constrictor" coiled around him from neck to waist; his friend wore colorful "slippers" on his feet. Their rowdy shipmates might get into fistfights with men from other vessels, have run-ins with local police, or drink themselves silly in a waterfront bar.

A bluejacket who returned to ship "drunk and dirty"

was disciplined by the captain. Gone were the days when discipline meant whipping or being "dropped from a yard," tossed into the sea from the top of a mast with a rope tied around the waist. Those guilty of ordinary offenses went to the "pie wagon," or ship's prison cell, for a week on hardtack and water. Stealing, however, was no ordinary offense. A thief was a lowlife who betrayed his mates. Such a person might easily turn tail in battle, letting them down at a critical moment. If caught stealing, a sailor was made to stand before the crew, the hatband with the ship's name in gold torn off, and then he was put ashore to look after himself. That was a harsh sentence, sometimes equivalent to a death order. It was one thing to be put ashore in an American or European port, but quite another to be abandoned in a place like Shanghai in China. There a foreigner without friends or money was a goner. Hoodlums might rob him of everything, including his clothes, or slit his throat in a back alley.

As commander in chief, President McKinley headed all United States military forces. Upon taking office, he chose John D. Long as Secretary of the Navy. Long, a former governor of Massachusetts, was a calm, softspoken man who hated war. The same could not be said of his assistant, a human dynamo who loved a good fight. His name was Theodore Roosevelt.

Born to a wealthy New York family in 1858, Roosevelt was destined to become one of the giants of American history. Theodore—he hated the nickname "Teddy"— had been a weak, sickly child who didn't seem long for this world. Fearing for his life, his father built a gymnasium at home and started him on regular exercises. He ran, did push-ups, worked out on the parallel bars, and learned to box. Boxing was his favorite sport, and while a student at Harvard University he became school champion. Upon graduation, he returned home, where he attended law school and married. His father having died by then, the couple lived with Mother Roosevelt in a large house on East 20th Street, and Theodore was elected to the New York legislature in 1882.

Life seemed perfect until tragedy struck in 1884. One morning in February, his mother died of typhoid fever. That same evening, his wife died in childbirth on the floor above. T.R., as friends called him, was heartbroken. In order to pull himself together, he went west, where he bought a ranch on the Little Missouri River in North Dakota. There he built a log house, mostly by himself, and learned about cattle. He enjoyed big game hunting so much that a friend said, "He wants to be killing something all the time."

At first, the cowboys didn't know what to make of the stranger. His upper-class accent and thick glasses made him seem a sissy and a dude. He quickly set them straight with a display of "fisticuffs." When a gunslinging bully crossed his path, T.R. flattened him with one punch and then showed him the way out of town. Because of his large teeth and odd laugh, the Indians called him "Laughing Horse"; cowboys called him "Toothadore." He'd laugh by setting his jaws, baring his teeth, and letting go with a loud "Hah!" If he really liked something, he'd cry, "Bully!" or "Capital!" He never forgot his two years on the Little Missouri or the friends he'd made there. Nor did they forget him. One day, as Rough Riders, they'd help drive the Spaniards from Cuba.

Roosevelt returned East in 1886 to continue his career

in politics. That year he ran unsuccessfully for mayor of New York. In the years that followed, he served as U.S. Civil Service Commissioner and as New York City Police Commissioner. Success in these posts, and the backing of political friends, brought him to the attention of the new president. When McKinley took office, he named T.R. Assistant Secretary of the Navy.

T.R. was a natural for the post. Ever since childhood, he'd been fascinated by the sea. Soon after leaving college, he wrote *The Naval War of 1812,* which became an overnight bestseller. His accounts of heroes such as Joshua Barney and the exploits of ships like "Old Ironsides" still make fascinating reading. Roosevelt's own favorite author was Alfred Thayer Mahan, the naval scholar. He read everything Mahan wrote and wrote him long personal letters. Mahan considered T.R. a genius and expected great things of him. He was not disappointed.

Roosevelt believed in the "strenuous life," that one must constantly exert oneself or go flabby and soft. Exertion, however, meant different things to different people. For individuals, it meant athletics and outdoor living. For nations, it meant war. T.R. insisted that war was beneficial to humanity. It strengthened a nation's moral fiber, enabling it to compete in the world. He said during a speech in 1897:

All the great masterful races have been fighting races; and the minute that a race loses the hard fighting virtues, then . . . it has lost its proud right to stand as the equal of the best. . . . A wealthy nation is an easy prey for any people that still retains the most valuable of all qualities, the soldierly qualities. . . . Peace is a goddess only when she comes with sword girt on thigh. . . . Cowardice in a race, as in an individual, is an unpardonable sin. . . . No triumph of peace is quite so great as the supreme triumphs of war. . . . It may be that at some time in the dim future of the race the need for war will vanish; but that time is yet ages distant. As yet no nation can hold its place in the world, or can do any work really worth doing, unless it stands ready to guard its rights with an armed hand.

This was the gospel that guided him during every day of his life.

As Assistant Secretary of the Navy, T.R. prepared for the war he hoped was coming. He was the first to realize that a war with Spain could not be fought in the Caribbean alone, but wherever Spanish seapower was found. Since the Philippine Islands were Spain's main base in the Pacific area, he believed they must be attacked as soon as hostilities began. The big day was coming, and he wanted to be ready. And readiness meant having the right men for the job. Quietly, so as not to alarm his superiors, he began shifting naval commanders to key posts.

The most capable of these was Commodore George Dewey. Aged sixty-one, Dewey had a white mustache and a ready smile. Those who didn't know him might take him for a kindly uncle. Those who did know him made no such mistake. Dewey, they said, had "fire in his belly." A veteran of the Civil War, he'd served under Admiral David Glasgow Farragut, who'd battered the Confederates all along the Mississippi River. Farragut was his hero, and he tried to be like him in every way.

Dewey had all of Farragut's drive and hot temper. He had once faced a mutiny of sailors aboard a vessel he commanded.

"Call the roll," he ordered.

"John Johnson," the clerk read from his list.

Silence.

"John Johnson, I see you," Dewey snapped. "I'm going to have your name called once more, and if you don't go on deck you will be a dead man."

"John Johnson."

More silence. Without batting an eyelash, Dewey whipped out a pistol and fired. John Johnson crumpled and lay in a pool of blood. "Now, men, the roll will be continued. As each name is called, you will answer and go on deck." And that is exactly what happened.

George Dewey was a man after T.R.'s heart. When the chief of the Pacific Squadron retired in December 1897, T.R. had Dewey appointed in his place. Two months later, the *Maine* exploded in Havana harbor.

On February 25, Secretary Long had a toothache. Leaving T.R. to run the office, he went to the dentist, then home for the rest of the day. Roosevelt, in charge at last, lost no time in putting the navy on a war footing. Huge supplies of ammunition were ordered. Ships were assigned to new stations. Congress was asked to allow more seamen to be recruited. Finally he sent a brief telegram to Dewey:

ORDER THE SQUADRON . . . TO HONG KONG. KEEP FULL OF COAL. IN THE EVENT OF DECLARATION OF WAR SPAIN, YOUR DUTY WILL BE TO SEE THAT THE SPANISH SQUADRON DOES NOT LEAVE THE ASIATIC COAST, AND THEN [BEGIN] OFFENSIVE OPERATIONS IN PHILIPPINE ISLANDS. . . .

ROOSEVELT.

A busy day's work! Although the nation was still at peace, T.R. had issued the first orders of the Spanish-American War.

Dewey followed instructions to the letter. When the actual war order arrived on April 26, his squadron was ready at Hong Kong, the British colony on the China coast. Proudly, the American vessels steamed out of the harbor past rows of British warships. The British crews wished them a safe voyage with blaring whistles and clanging bells.

Yet their cheerful farewell masked deep concern. "A fine set of fellows," Englishmen told one another, "but unhappily we shall never see them again." They were sure that the feisty Dewey had bitten off more than he could chew; the Yanks were sailing to their doom. Everyone knew that the Spaniards had built strong defenses in the Philippines. Manila, the islands' capital and chief city, was supposed to be a fortress. Months before, the Spaniards had made a show of mining the entrance to Manila Bay. Batteries of heavy guns guarded the city's approaches. Worst of all, the Spanish Pacific Fleet rode at anchor, ready for action.

Dewey may have had fire in his belly, but his mind was cool and calm. He knew of the Englishmen's concerns, but did not take them seriously. Before leaving Washington, he'd collected every scrap of information he could find about the Philippines. In addition, he had Naval intelligence agents interview people who'd recently visited the islands. After giving careful thought to Manila's defenses, he decided that there was little to fear. The mines were probably old models and, by now, fouled by seaweed; it

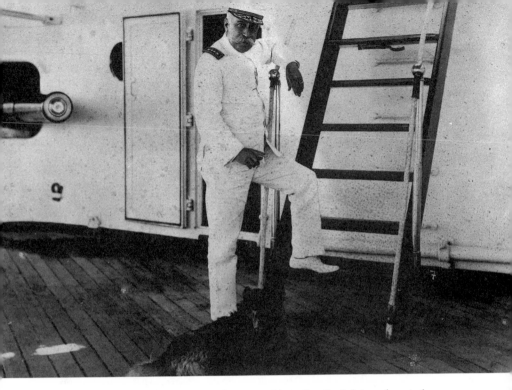

Admiral George Dewey on the deck of the Olympia. *Notice that the deck is made, not of steel, but of wooden planks. Although these saved weight, allowing the ship to go faster, they could easily catch fire during a battle.*

would be a miracle if any exploded. Shore batteries were certainly dangerous, but they'd never stopped Farragut, and they wouldn't stop him. The Spanish fleet, which should have been his biggest worry, seemed like a pack of toothless sharks. He'd learned that it consisted of two cruisers and five gunboats, vessels of about a thousand tons mounting light, quick-firing cannon. The ships were old and in poor condition. Their crews, who'd had target practice only once during the past year, weren't looking forward to battle with *los Américanos.*

Dewey, however, commanded four modern cruisers, two gunboats, and a cutter, a fast vessel used for carrying messages. His men, trained to a razor-sharp edge, were raring for a fight. As far as he was concerned, they were sailing not to a battle, but to a military execution.

The squadron steamed southward across the South China Sea. Dewey, never one to waste time, kept his crews busy from dawn to dusk. There were constant drills. Sometimes bugles sounded "General Quarters" at midnight, causing men to leap from hammocks in their underwear and race barefoot to their battle stations. Guns were polished with care; gunners felt close to their weapons, on which their lives depended, and gave them pet names such as "Netty" and "Honey." Every bit of wood that could be spared was tossed overboard to lessen the danger of fire. Ditty boxes, tables, benches, chairs, and decorative wall panels bobbed in the wake of each vessel. Men went about their work so enthusiastically that they threw their own mess gear overboard and had to eat off their laps for weeks afterward.

On the second day out, captains read their crews a notice from the Spanish governor of the Philippines. It had come into Dewey's hands the day before sailing, and he wanted to share it with his men. In it the governor, who surely had a way with words, called the Americans cowards, drunkards, liars, thieves, scoundrels, murderers, kidnappers, and enemies of religion. "The aggressors . . . shall not profane the tombs of your fathers," he'd told his troops. "They shall not gratify their lustful passions on your wives' and daughters' honor. . . ."

This nonsense may have cheered the Spaniards, but it made the Americans fighting mad. After reading the notice, one captain threw it on deck, stomped on it, and cursed its author. Ships' bands struck up "Yankee Doodle" and "Marching Through Georgia," a rousing Civil War tune. And, of course, the men sang "There'll Be a Hot Time in the Old Town Tonight!"

On the night of April 30, the moon outlined a dark mass on the horizon: Luzon, largest of the Philippine Islands. Dewey signaled a halt and called his captains aboard his flagship, the cruiser *Olympia,* for last-minute orders.

"Very well, gentlemen," he said. "We shall enter Manila Bay tonight and you will follow the motions and movements of the flagship, which will lead." That was it. There was no discussion and no questions. There was nothing to talk about. Dewey was about to live out the great dream of his life. Like Farragut, he'd find the enemy, lead his ships to him, and fight him to the death.

As the meeting ended, Dewey's nephew, Lieutenant William Winder, stepped forward and snapped a salute. "Commodore, I have always made it a policy never to take advantage of our being related," he said firmly. "But in this instance I should like to make an exception." He believed the channel into Manila Bay was mined and wanted to lead the way in. "Sir, this is the one chance I have to become famous."

Dewey understood. He stood silently for a minute, smiling.

"Billy, I have waited sixty years for this opportunity. And much as I like you and know you are a fine officer . . . mines or no mines, I am leading the squadron in myself. Good luck, my boy."

Slowly the darkened ships, each with only a single stern light to show its presence, formed a line of battle. *Olympia* led the way, followed by the crusiers *Baltimore* and *Raleigh,* the gunboats *Petrel* and *Concord,* the cruiser *Boston,* and the cutter *McCulloch.* Gongs gave the signal to "Clear for Action!"

It was the same aboard each ship in the squadron. Watertight doors were slammed shut, sealing the vessel into compartments that would keep it afloat even if several of them were flooded. Battle hatches, heavy slabs of iron, were placed over hatches topside to prevent fires from traveling downward. Rope nets, each strand as thick as a man's finger, were hung around exposed places to catch flying splinters. Loose deck gear—gangplanks, paint buckets, mops—went overboard. Firemen hosed down decks and covered lifeboats with wet canvas. Engineers sent jets of compressed air over coals to increase boiler pressure and speed. Gunners tested the turret-turning machinery. Shell boys brought ammunition from the magazines and piled it near the guns. In the sick bay, surgeons and their assistants laid out instruments, bandages, and drugs and covered the operating tables with rubber sheets. Two buckets were placed on the floor next to each table—one for blood, the other for amputated limbs. The dead would be thrown overboard; ships in action were busy places, and bodies got in the way. Besides, the sight of mangled bodies might cause panic among the living.

During the first minutes of Sunday, May 1, the squadron steamed toward Manila Bay. All was quiet, save for the thumping of the ships' engines. To the left, dimly outlined against the sky, lookouts saw a tadpole-shaped island: Corregidor. To the right lay El Fraile Island—the Friar. Both had powerful shore batteries manned by Spanish soldiers. The Spaniards were at their posts, since they expected the Americans. Before sailing, one of the reporters aboard the *Olympia* had cabled Dewey's plans to the *New York World*. Pulitzer, eager to scoop his enemy

Hearst, printed the story. No matter that the news would be in Spanish hands within twenty-four hours.

Six of the ships entered Manila Bay without being noticed. But just as the last vessel, the *McCulloch,* passed Corregidor, a pillar of flame leaped from her smokestack. Soot had caught fire, alerting the Spaniards.

Suddenly, a rocket went up from Corregidor, rose on a silvery trail, and burst into a red ball of fire. For a moment the area became clear as day, revealing the American squadron. The gunners on El Fraile opened fire, but they were poor marksmen, and their shells exploded harmlessly.

"Well, well," said Dewey, turning to Captain Charles V. Gridley of the *Olympia.* "They did wake up at last."

Boston, Concord, Raleigh, and *McCulloch* immediately returned the enemy's fire. After a three-minute volley, the battery on El Fraile fell silent. No mines exploded.

The Americans entered Manila Bay and headed for the city on its eastern shore. Yet Dewey was in no hurry. Once clear of El Fraile, he signaled his ships to slow down to four knots. There was still five hours to dawn, and he didn't want to reach Manila before daybreak. He wanted to choose his targets carefully rather than waste ammunition in a night battle.

At 5:00 A.M. Manila came into view just as the sun rose. Scores of merchant ships rode at anchor between the American squadron and the city. But Spanish warships were nowhere to be seen. Admiral Montojo, the Spanish fleet commander, was a true gentleman. Knowing that the city would be damaged if a battle was fought so close to shore, he'd sent his ships to the naval base of Cavite a few miles south.

With no enemy in sight, Dewey tensed up, until the lookout turned his binoculars toward Cavite. Then, signal flags were hoisted on *Olympia*'s mast, ordering the squadron to head for the naval base. As it swung past Manila, Spanish shore batteries opened fire. Once again, however, the gunners weren't up to their job. The heavy shells flew wide of the mark, without so much as scratching an American ship.

Cavite is on a peninsula shaped like a lobster claw. The base was protected by heavy guns overlooking the harbor, with the area enclosed by the "claw." Montojo's ships were anchored across the mouth of the harbor. Rather than maneuver in open water, he'd decided to use them as if they were stationary forts. Although he expected to put up a fierce fight, he didn't expect to win. Indeed, his ships were anchored in shallow water so that their crews could cling to the wreckage until rescued.

The Americans, advancing in line, were unable to bring their guns to bear for nearly a half-hour. The Spanish ships, facing them broadside, had a clear field of fire, and their gunners cut loose with everything they had. Geysers of water splashed on either side of the oncoming ships; shells burst overhead, spraying decks with chunks of hot metal.

Enemy fire was increasing when Dewey signaled, "Prepare for General Action." His men had crossed the world for this moment. Instantly, Old Glory rose to the masthead of every ship in the squadron. Ship's bands, assembled topside to cheer the fighters, struck up "The Star-Spangled Banner." Officers and men did as they'd always done when the national anthem was played. Those on deck stood at attention and saluted as if on parade. Then they gave their battle cry: "Remember the *Maine!*" Those in the turrets took up the cry and checked their guns for the last time. Cavite lay straight ahead.

At exactly 5:41 A.M., Dewey called to *Olympia*'s captain. In a loud, clear voice that was overheard by scores of men, he said: "You may fire when you are ready, Gridley."

Olympia's eight-inch rifles roared into action. Seconds later, every gun in the squadron was blazing away.

As the Americans steamed past the Spanish line, they came about, crossed their own wakes, and returned for another pass. The men in the gun turrets lost track of time once they got into the swing of things. Each gun became a living being and they existed only to push "food" into its yawning mouth.

"Load!" shouted the gun captain. A warhead followed by a bag of powder slid into the breech, the opening behind the barrel, and the breech lock closed behind it.

"Point!" The aimers spun their wheels, turning the massive weapon with a twist of the wrist.

"Fire!" The explosion set off shock waves that bounced off the steel walls, striking the men's ears like hard fists; anyone who forgot to stuff his ears with cotton might become permanently deaf.

"Sponge!" A damp sponge at the end of a long pole was rammed into the smoking breech. Particles of burning powder often clung to the inside of the barrel. Inserting a fresh powder charge without sponging might cause the gun to explode, killing everyone in the turret.

"Load!"

Unlike the Spaniards, who used smokeless powder, a recent invention, the Americans still used black powder, which gave off clouds of smoke. That made the gunners' jobs harder. Smoke built up faster in the turret than it could be expelled by the ventilators, filling the area with a grayish haze. The gunners coughed and sneezed; their eyes stung and tears flowed. Heat built up, forcing them to shed their shirts and pants; finally they took off their underwear, standing naked except for their shoes. Particles of gunpowder clung to their bodies, turning them black, except for the white streaks revealed by rivulets of sweat. Every twenty minutes mess boys brought whiskey and water to keep up their energy. Some grew tipsy and began to sing, or curse, as they went about their work. Dewey had given orders against profanity, but no one, himself included, obeyed them.

Yet the gun turrets were paradise compared to the engine rooms. Pandemonium ruled in those narrow, low-ceilinged compartments. The clattering of the engines and the roaring of the furnaces made it seem as if one's head would burst at any moment. The black gangs stood before the open furnaces, shoveling coal as fast as they could. Temperatures soared, reaching 200° Fahrenheit! "We don't have to worry," said one stoker, "for Hell ain't no hotter than this!"

Stoker Charles H. Twitchell of the *Olympia* always remembered that day:

The battle hatches were all battened down, and we were shut in this little hole. . . . it was so hot our hair was singed. There were several leaks in the steam pipes, and the hissing hot steam made things worse. . . . We could tell when our guns opened fire by the way the ship shook; we could scarcely stand on our feet, the vibration was so great. . . . The ship shook so fearfully that the soot and cinders poured down on us in clouds. Now and then a big drop of scalding water would fall on our bare heads, and the pain was intense. One by one three of our men were overcome by the terrible heat and were hoisted to the upper deck.

The Americans fired often and well. Although the enemy fought with desperate courage, the Spanish ships soon became floating slaughterhouses. Powder magazines exploded. Chunks of steel buzz-sawed through the air, slicing through anything that stood in their way. Puddles of blood and pieces of flesh littered the decks. The wounded lay everywhere, moaning or screaming in pain. Eighty men lay in the infirmary of the *Cristina,* Montojo's flagship, attended by overworked doctors. There were many close calls, until an eight-inch shell from the *Olympia* burst through the ship's side and exploded. No

Stokers of the "black gang" feed coal into the boilers of the Olympia *during the Battle of Manila Bay.*

one after that, patient or doctor, needed or could give medical attention. All were blown apart or burned alive in the fire that swept the infirmary.

The Americans had begun their fifth pass when Dewey learned that ammunition was dangerously low. At 7:35 A.M., he ordered the squadron to pull back for an ammunition count and to serve breakfast to the men, who hadn't eaten since the night before. The sailors, thinking the break was merely for food, weren't shy about voicing their opinion. "For God's sake, Captain," a gunner aboard the *Boston* yelled, "don't let us stop now! To hell with breakfast!" Nevertheless, they appreciated the meal and the rest.

Dewey reviewed the messages sent by his captains. There had been an error in earlier communications. Not only was there enough ammunition, but the ships had suffered little damage. There were few wounded, none of them seriously. The only death was the *McCulloch*'s chief engineer, who'd suffered a heart attack brought on by the heat in the engine room.

After a two-hour break, the American ships moved in for the kill. But by then there was little left to do. By 11:00 A.M. every Spanish warship was either burning, sunk, or sinking. Dewey signaled the *Petrel,* which could sail in shallow water, to move in and finish the job. Damaged warships were blown up. Supply ships and transports anchored in the harbor were put to the torch. The *Petrel* then pounded Cavite's shore batteries until the Spaniards hauled down their colors and raised a white bedsheet in surrender.

All through the battle Manila's shore batteries had lobbed shells at the Americans; however, early in the

The destruction of the Spanish fleet at Manila Bay as shown in a Russian print of 1898.

afternoon Dewey ordered *Olympia, Baltimore,* and *Raleigh* to anchor just outside the city in clear view of the defenders. A longboat was sent ashore with a message: If one more shot came his way, Dewey promised to blast Manila to rubble. The Spanish guns immediately ceased fire.

That night, as the American squadron lay offshore, *Olympia*'s band played "La Paloma" ("The Dove"), a Spanish favorite. It was a sign of goodwill, and Manila's citizens took it as such. Hundreds came to the beach to admire the sleek warships and thank Heaven that their city had been spared. *"Américanos siempre caballeros!"* they called to the waving bluejackets. "Americans are always gentlemen!"

Dewey could scarcely believe his eyes when he read the battle figures. The Battle of Manila Bay had cost the

Spaniards their entire fleet, plus 167 seamen killed and 214 wounded. American losses were one dead (*McCulloch*'s engineer) and eight wounded. His ships were only slightly damaged—nothing that his repair crews couldn't handle.

The Commodore went to bed that night a happy man. He'd achieved his life's ambition. He was the new Farragut.

News of Dewey's victory took the United States by surprise. Few Americans had ever heard of the Philippines, let alone knew anything about them. Mr. Dooley, a popular comic character, spoke for his fellow countrymen: He couldn't decide whether they were islands or canned goods.* Even President McKinley was confused. "Before the battle I could not have told where those darned islands were within two thousand miles!" he admitted to a White House guest.

Commodore Dewey became the hero of the hour. Nothing was too good for him. The President showed his appreciation by promoting him to Rear Admiral. Congress, not to be outdone, gave him a sword with a gold handle and the initials "G.D.U.S.N." studded in diamonds. Cities named avenues, streets, and schools in his honor.

The American people simply went wild. Wherever you went, his image followed you. It stared from Dewey dolls, Dewey beer mugs, Dewey paperweights, Dewey inkwells, Dewey spoons, Dewey buttons, Dewey medals,

*Finley Peter Dunne wrote a widely read newspaper column under the name of Mr. Dooley. A bartender by profession, Mr. Dooley combined wisdom with humor in a thick Irish brogue.

and countless other Dewey doodads. His picture appeared on soap wrappers—proof of the benefits of cleanliness. A laxative bore his name; "the salt of salts," according to the advertisement. Songs like "Dewey's Duty Done," "What Did Dewey Do to Them?" and "How Did Dewey Do It?" became hits. Hundreds of poems, mostly awful, celebrated the man and his deed. The most famous poem was written by "Ironquill" and first appeared in a Topeka, Kansas, newspaper:

> *Oh, dewy was the morning,*
> *Upon the first of May,*
> *And Dewey was the admiral,*
> *Down in Manila Bay.*
> *And dewy were the Spaniards' eyes,*
> *Them orbs of royal blue,*
> *And dew we feel discouraged?*
> *I dew not think we dew!*

Down in Manila Bay, the Admiral had his hands full. Foreign warships began to arrive within days of his victory. He expected them, since it was customary for neutral commanders to view a battle scene and report to their home governments afterward. The British came first, followed by the French and Japanese. Since the Spaniards refused to surrender the city, Dewey had been forced to set up a naval blockade. Under international law, it was his right to establish rules for visiting ships, and there were no problems. The visitors recognized Dewey's authority and obeyed his rules without question. Then the Germans arrived.

In mid-May, Admiral Otto von Diedrichs led a squadron into Manila Bay. Composed of three cruisers and two battleships, it was far more powerful than Dewey's squadron. The German government, eager for bases in the Pacific, had sent von Diedrichs on a delicate mission. He was to intimidate the Americans, forcing them to withdraw. Then, if the Philippines could be taken without difficulty, he was to do it. He must not, however, start a war with the United States.

Von Diedrichs began to test American determination. His ships steamed in an out of the American formation, sometimes getting too close for comfort. If ordered to stop and identify themselves, they'd blow their foghorns and keep going. During the day, they saluted the Spanish flag and ignored Old Glory. At night, they turned on their searchlights, revealing the American positions to the enemy. Food and other supplies were given to the Spaniards, along with promises that Germany would stand by them no matter what happened.

Dewey was not the sort of man to overlook an insult. One day in June, von Diedrichs sent a lieutenant aboard the *Olympia* with an important message. The young man clicked his heels and began to recite his lines. He'd come to protest the American blockade rules. They were unfair and had to change immediately, he said. Dewey listened quietly—*too* quietly. His aides stood by grim-faced, waiting. They knew the danger signs: The more his anger grew, the quieter he became, until he erupted like a volcano.

When the German finished, Dewey stared at him for a few minutes without speaking. You could hear a pin drop. Then the words came.

"Does 'His Excellency' [von Diedrichs] know that it is my force and not his which is blockading this port?"

"Yes, sir," replied the lieutenant.

"And is he aware that he has no rights here except those I choose to allow him?"

The lieutenant shrugged his shoulders.

"One would imagine, sir, that you were conducting this blockade."

Again he shrugged. He was an arrogant fellow and not easily ruffled.

"Do you want war with us?" Dewey shouted, his faced flushed, the veins bulging in his throat.

That shook the lieutenant. "Certainly not," he said.

"Well, it looks like it. And you are very near it; and you can have it, sir, as soon as you like."

Then he pointed to the cabin door and turned away. Dismissed! The interview was over.

"Mein Gott! Mein Gott!" ["My God! My God!"] the German stammered, as he left the *Olympia.* That American was a lunatic.

Although von Diedrichs promptly mended his ways, Dewey had formed his opinion of Germany. He detested that country and predicted that, some day, America would have to fight it. He was right.

But that day was still nineteen years in the future. Meantime, the blockade went smoothly, while Washington decided what to do about the Philippines.

▯▯▯
Marching Off to War

"God takes care of children, drunkards, and the United States of America."

—*An old saying*

President McKinley awoke early one morning and went into his White House office. Closing the door, he sat alone for a long time behind the large desk, thinking—worrying. There was plenty to worry about. The navy had just won a magnificent victory due to daring, skill, and modern equipment. The army, however, was another matter. It was unprepared for a major war; indeed, it hardly existed at all.

In May 1898, the United States Army numbered exactly 28,183 officers and men. Known as "doughboys," from "adobe," the white clay that covered marching troops in desert country, man for man they were the equal of any soldiers on Earth. For the past thirty years they had been stationed at outposts scattered across the Great Plains and the Southwest. One by one, they'd defeated the American Indian tribes that had ruled those lands for centuries. Sioux, Cheyenne, Comanche, Apache, and others were broken and herded onto reservations. Geronimo the Apache, last of the great war chiefs, was captured in 1886. The army's last campaign ended four years later with the massacre of a Sioux band at Wounded Knee, South Dakota.

Americans were satisfied with their army. True, it was small, nothing compared to the European armies. But it did its job well and, best of all, at little cost to the taxpayer. The United States was not Europe. Ever since the days of George Washington, the U.S. had no "entangling alliances," no obligations to fight for foreigners in distant lands. America threatened no country, and no country threatened America. Why have a big army if there wasn't a big enemy to fight? The very idea seemed ridiculous.

When an enemy did appear—Spain—it became clear that the army had serious problems. Inexperience was the rule rather than the exception. Except for aging veterans of the Civil War, no officer had ever led a large unit in battle. The army had no war plans, no general staff to make such plans, and no training in landing troops on a defended coast. Basic information was simply unavailable. Army intelligence, someone said half-jokingly, should be renamed "Army ignorance." There were no accurate maps of Cuba, and the main source of information was a book by an officer who'd never visited the place. No one knew how many Spanish troops were on the island or their exact location. Luckily for the soldiers, most Spaniards would be too busy chasing guerrillas to meet the invaders when they came ashore.

Essential equipment was either in short supply or lacking entirely. There were never enough wagons, or mules to pull them. Troopships? The army had none; it eventually rented passenger ships, cargo vessels, and cattle boats to use as transports. Although a war in Cuba had been discussed for years, it never occurred to the War Department that Americans might have to fight in a tropical climate. That was a major oversight, especially for the soldiers. Their uniforms, designed for use on the Great Plains, consisted of cowhide boots, felt hats, heavy blue woolen shirts and pants, and long flannel underwear. Photos show that "longjohns" were worn even in the Cuban jungle. These uniforms would eventually cause almost as much suffering as enemy bullets.

Weapons were another problem. The War Department favored the Krag-Jörgensen rifle. Known as the "Krag," it was a five-shot repeater that weighed nearly eleven pounds and used smokeless powder, which allowed a man to shoot from cover without being seen. American artillery, however, still used black powder, which created clouds of smoke and gave away their position. That was no problem on the open sea, where thick smoke might hide a moving vessel from enemy gunners. But on land, smoke attracted enemy fire, causing needless losses. The Spaniards had learned their lesson while fighting the guerrillas. Their troops were equipped with German-made weapons, perhaps the finest in the world at that time. Their Krupp cannon were easy to aim, fired quickly, and used smokeless powder. Their Mauser rifles were lightweight and held eleven smokeless-powder bullets.

In addition to the regular army, about one hundred thousand Americans belonged to the National Guard. Unfortunately, there was nothing "national" about the guard except its name. Each state had its own guard, which served as the governor's private army when needed. During natural disasters, for example, a governor would call out the guard to keep order and aid the victims. During strikes and riots, it served as a reserve police force. Guardsmen saw themselves as something special. They elected their officers, wore their state uniforms, and owed their loyalty to their state, not to the federal government.

Guard training was little more than parading on holidays and firing a few shots each summer. Since there weren't enough Krags to go around, guardsmen relied on the Springfield rifle. This Civil War relic had a short range and fired one shot at a time. It took a strong man to handle a Springfield. "Each cartridge," a private recalled, "was as big as your finger. . . . It could, properly directed, knock down two men, the one it hit and the one who fired it. . . . It had . . . old-fashioned black powder, and with each discharge, there burst forth a cloud of white smoke somewhat the size of a cow."

When President McKinley asked guardsmen to join the army, they turned him down flat. Army service meant accepting army discipline and, as one guardsman explained: "To fight for my country as a volunteer in a regiment I love would be a glorious pleasure, but to serve in the Regular Army and do chores . . . well, I would rather be executed!" McKinley solved the problem through a compromise. Any guard unit that enlisted could keep its elected officers.

There were all sorts of schemes for creating volunteer units. "Buffalo Bill" Cody, the old Indian fighter and showman, promised to kick the Spaniards out of Cuba with thirty thousand "Indian braves." Frank James, who'd ridden the outlaw trail with his brother Jesse, offered to lead a regiment of cowboys. It was said that the Sioux were ready to go on the warpath and take Spanish scalps. Mrs. Martha A. Shute of Denver, Colorado, wanted to form a troop of cavalry made up entirely of women. Willie Hearst suggested a regiment of all-star athletes: prizefighters, wrestlers, baseball players, football players, rowers, runners, gymnasts. Our athletes, he boasted, were practically bulletproof. They "would overawe any Spanish regiment by their mere appearance. They would scorn . . . Mauser bullets."

The President ignored these harebrained schemes. Instead, he called for 125,000 volunteers, including three volunteer cavalry regiments of a thousand men each. Americans were suddenly gripped by "volunteer fever." Wives bid tearful farewell to their husbands. Children waved good-bye to their fathers. Young women urged their beaux to enlist. The air filled with snappy songs like "On To Cuba":

> On to Cuba! On to Cuba!
>   Sound the war note high and shrill,
>   Rescue from the vulture tyrant
>   City, village, plain and hill. . . .
>   As ye charge across the plain,
>   Smite to earth the Spanish coyote;
>   Slay! in vengeance for the Maine.

A million men flocked to the recruiting stations. Desperate to serve, they'd do anything to pass the physical examination. One fellow drank a gallon of water to meet the minimum weight requirement. Another fellow, undersized by three-eighths of an inch, lay in bed for three

New York street scene, 1898. Passersby read a poster outside an army recruiting station, in this case a post office on lower Broadway. A corporal looks on, eager to invite them inside to sign the enlistment papers.

days in the hope of "lengthening" his body. It didn't help, and 77 percent of all volunteers were rejected.

The luckiest were accepted into the First United States Volunteer Cavalry Regiment. As soon as Congress gave its approval, Secretary of War Russell A. Alger invited Theodore Roosevelt to become the unit's colonel. T.R. refused, claiming lack of military experience. However, he accepted the rank of lieutenant colonel when the Secretary offered to name his friend Leonard Wood colonel.

Wood, T.R.'s junior by two years, was an avid sportsman; he especially liked boxing and sailing small boats in rough weather. After graduating from Harvard Medical School, he enlisted in the army. Sent to the Southwest,

Although Colonel Leonard Wood officially commanded the Rough Riders, everyone knew that Theodore Roosevelt was its true leader.

he quickly earned a reputation for skill and daring. Not only was he an excellent surgeon, he was a fine soldier, winning the Medal of Honor for leading raids against the Apaches. He later went to Washington as President McKinley's personal physician.

T.R. and Wood made a perfect team. Between the two of them, they knew all the "right" people in Washington. These were government officials who knew where scarce equipment could be found and how to bend the rules to get it. Within two weeks, while the regiment was still forming, it received the best of everything. Trainloads of supplies were rushed to its training camp in San Antonio, Texas. There were plenty of horses—for the First Volunteer Cavalry. Its troopers were given tan cotton uniforms, not the regular-issue sweatsuits. Best of all, it was the only volunteer unit to be issued the Krag.

T.R. wanted the regiment to represent the "best" elements in American life. This meant basically two types of recruit. The first he termed the "gilded gang." Men like himself, they were wealthy and educated, eager for a good fight in the service of their country. A list of their names reads like the Social Register. Among them were men whose families had come on the *Mayflower* or had served Peter Stuyvesant when he'd governed New Amsterdam for the Dutch. There were graduates of Harvard and other Ivy League schools, a national tennis champion, a world-champion polo player, and members of exclusive New York social clubs. There were bankers, stockbrokers, and lawyers wise in the ways of Wall Street. Roosevelt made it clear that they weren't going on a joyride. War was serious business, and he expected them to act like soldiers. Although they had servants at home, as buck privates they'd have to take orders and do hard, dirty work without complaint. According to Roosevelt, anyone who thought otherwise needn't sign up, but once he did, there could be no backing out. And not a man backed out or failed to do his duty.

The backbone of the regiment, however, were the types of men Roosevelt had known during his ranching days. These were the westerners, sons and grandsons of the pioneers. A colorful lot, they went by such nicknames as "Cherokee Bill," "Happy Jack," "Dead Shot Jim," "Lariat Ned," "Rattlesnake Pete," "Weeping Dutchman,"

"Prayerful James," and "Rubber Shoe Andy," supposedly the noisiest man on two feet.

Roosevelt's men hailed from the Rockies and the Dakota Badlands. There were Texans, New Mexicans, Oklahomans, and Coloradans. Robert Brown, who'd shot five men in "righteous" causes, reached San Antonio by way of Arizona's Skull Valley, Devil's Gate, and Dead Man's Gulch. The regiment boasted eight sheriffs, seven army deserters, and an unreported number of outlaws. Marshal Ben Daniels of Dodge City came from the toughest cowtown in the West. Charlie Younger was the son of Bob Younger of the Jesse James gang. Charlie bunked with cowboys, broncobusters, buffalo hunters, Indians and Indian fighters. Most were bowlegged and all were more comfortable on horseback than walking. When eighteen-year-old Jess Langdon was asked if he could ride a horse, he said with a snort: "I can ride anything that's got hair on it!"

At first the volunteers were disappointed with their colonel. Wood came to be known as "Old Poker Face," because he seldom smiled or showed his feelings. A stickler for discipline, he wanted things done "by the book." The men learned that there were three ways of doing things: the right way, the wrong way, and the army way. And the army way was Wood's way. Anyone who didn't toe the mark got an earful of army language that would make a top sergeant cringe, followed by a few days of peeling potatoes or tidying up around camp.

There was also a fourth way—T.R.'s way. Roosevelt was a natural leader. Upon arriving in camp, he began to memorize the men's names; before the week was out, he could match every name to a face. While Wood saw that things ran smoothly, T.R. put the troopers through their paces. That wasn't easy, since he had to learn by trial and error. At the beginning, it was mostly error. He'd sit atop his favorite horse, Little Texas, trying to form a skirmish line. His high-pitched voice rattled the horses and confused their riders. When he finally succeeded, the men didn't cheer or applaud. They blazed away with their six-shooters, causing a stampede.

T.R. believed in rewarding good work. Once, when a squadron did particularly well, he lined it up outside a tavern.

"Captains will let the men go in and drink all the beer they want, and I will pay for it," he announced.

Theodore Roosevelt as colonel of the Rough Riders. "T.R." may have spoken like a dude, but he was a tough, able leader who knew how to get the most from his men.

Then he shook his big fist and warned: "If any man drinks more beer than is good for him, I will cinch him!" No one did, for everyone knew that T.R. always kept his word.

Word of his generosity reached Wood almost immediately. The Colonel wasn't pleased, saying that any officer who treated his men to beer wasn't fit to be in the service.

That night, before taps, Roosevelt came to Wood's tent. Standing straight as a rail, he said: "I wish to say, sir, that I consider myself the damnedest ass within ten miles of this camp. Good night."

The troopers came to trust him, to *love* him, regarding him as their real leader. Wood realized this, but wasn't offended. He told friends that if the war lasted more than a few months, he expected to be "kicked upstairs" to make room for Roosevelt.

Meantime, T.R. was bursting with pride in his men. By the end of May, he'd forged them into a real fighting force. They could, he said modestly, "whip Caesar's Tenth Legion," the best unit in the Roman army. Perhaps. A visitor to their camp described them in a private letter:

> *If anyone thinks that Colonel Roosevelt got up this outfit to parade with, that person is a fool. . . . [They] are the toughest set of men I have ever met. Many of them are outlaws and I might venture that 70 percent of them are 'man killers' of some note in one part or another of the wild and wooly West. Their language is beyond description and they are always fighting and ready to shoot at the first chance that offers. They all carry 45-calibre six-shooters and knives. . . . On the other hand, they always stand ready to help a fellow out of any difficulty, and will share their last cent with you.*

Colonel Roosevelt and some of his Rough Rider officers at lunch at their camp outside San Antonio, Texas. The black butler to the right waits to take their orders.

Troopers showed their affection for T.R. by the names they chose for their regiment. The First United States Volunteer Cavalry was fine for official records, but dry as adobe dust. Men wanted a name that captured their daring, spirit, and eagerness to fight. They experimented with names like "Teddy's Terrors," "Teddy's Texas Tarantulas," "Teddy's Rustler Regiment," and "Roosevelt's Rough 'Uns." Finally they settled on "Roosevelt's Rough Riders"—Rough Riders for short. Thus the legend was born.

On May 28, 1898, a telegram arrived from Washington. Colonel Wood read it silently, then handed it to T.R. without comment. Suddenly they threw themselves into each others arms and began whooping like wildmen. The

Rough Riders had been ordered to Tampa, Florida. Located on the state's west coast, Tampa was the jumping-off point for the invasion of Cuba.

The regiment headed east and then south in seven flag-draped trains. Wherever it stopped along the route, it was greeted by crowds of well-wishers. Townspeople handed the sweaty men free watermelons and buckets of iced beer. Local drum-and-bugle corps made a racket that could wake the dead. Pretty girls in straw hats and bright gingham dresses blew them kisses. In their eyes, the Rough Riders were already heroes.

Black soldiers traveling the same route found a different reception. Their story goes back to the winning of the West after the Civil War. Beginning in 1865, thousands of blacks headed west in search of a better life. They easily fit into the life of the frontier; there was plenty to do, and employers weren't fussy about your background so long as you did a good day's work. Blacks became stagecoach drivers, mule skinners, and railroad men. Many worked on ranches as ropers, herdsmen, broncobusters, and trail cooks; about one in four cowboys was a former slave or the son of a slave. Without them, the cattle industry could never have prospered.

Other blacks became professional soldiers. Four black regiments—the Twenty-fourth and Twenty-fifth Infantry and the Ninth and Tenth Cavalry—served on the northern Plains and along the Mexican border. Although enlisted men were black, their officers were always white. White officers thought highly of their men; indeed, they were proud to lead them. For example, General John J. Pershing, commander of American forces in the First

World War, was called "Black Jack" because of his early service with black troops. White settlers praised the blacks' courage during the Indian wars. So did American Indians, who called them Buffalo Soldiers because their hair was like the coarse, knotted hair of the buffalo. Their heroism is indicated by the fact that between 1870 and 1890, fourteen blacks received the Medal of Honor, the nation's highest award.

When the Spanish war began, the black regiments were ordered to Florida. As they moved southward, local people turned out at stations along their route. The soldiers had been the people's protectors, and now people gave them a royal send-off. George W. Prioleau, a black chaplain, recalled the journey of the Ninth Cavalry: "All the way from northwest Nebraska this regiment was greeted with cheers and hurrahs. At places where we stopped the people assembled by the thousands. . . . The [troopers] would raise their hats, [while] men, women, and children would wave their handkerchiefs, and the heavens would resound to their hearty cheers. The white hand shaking the black hand."

The cheering stopped once the trains crossed the borders of the old Confederacy. Blacks who stood on the platforms were not allowed to approach the trains. Whites seemed not to notice them; and those who did had hatred in their eyes. The troopers were shocked. Out west, they'd never known such behavior. Gradually it dawned on them that although the Civil War had ended years before, these whites couldn't accept the fact that slavery was over.

The 1890s were a bleak time for most black Americans. It was a time of bigotry based on racism, the belief that

blacks were by nature inferior to whites. Racism, supposedly "scientific," was widely accepted in the United
States. It was taught in the schools, written about in the
newspapers, and had become a part of everyday life. Even
the *Encyclopedia Britannica* spread racist ideas. According
to the American edition of 1895, there was no doubt
about "the inherent mental inferiority of blacks." Racism,
of course, is not scientific; it is a dangerous myth that has
been used as an excuse for injustice.

Blacks were known by such insulting names as "niggers," "coons," "darkies." Since they were supposedly
inferior, they must be kept in their place by Jim Crow
laws. Jim Crow was another name for segregation; it
comes from a song about Jim, a happy slave as black as
the blackest crow. Throughout the South, blacks were
forbidden to attend "white" schools; railroad stations had
special "black" waiting rooms, water fountains, and toilets. Parks had signs tacked to trees: "No Niggers and
Dogs Allowed in Here." White shopkeepers needn't serve
black customers. Blacks were prevented from voting and
traveling freely. Those who became "uppity," or stood up
for their rights, were visited by the Ku Klux Klan, bullies
in white bedsheets who beat them, even killed them,
without fear of the law.

Southern blacks lived in terror. "They fear the white
man about as much as the rat does the cat," a black
trooper wrote from Macon, Georgia. "There is no law
here that a white man is bound to respect where our
people are concerned. The 'Negro' is looked upon as a
menial servant, with the epithet of 'nigger' and 'coon,'
and in return the whites expect to be addressed as 'marsa'
and 'misses'. . . . Surely there must be a just God who will

someday turn his lovingkindness on the Negro in the South."

Black soldiers were proud, self-respecting people. As soldiers, they were used to serving under whites. An officer would address a man as "Private So-and-so." In return, he'd salute and address him as "Sir." That was as it should be. But to be called "nigger" and have to answer "marsa"? That was degrading.

Black soldiers and white bigots were an explosive combination. Cafés and soda fountains that refused to serve blacks might be wrecked. In Key West, Florida, a black sergeant was arrested for refusing to hand over his pistol to the white sheriff; it was part of his uniform and he had every right to carry it. Upon hearing of the arrest, his men visited the jail with rifles and fixed bayonets. The sheriff "saw their point" and let the prisoner go. When a barber in Lakeland, Florida, refused to shave blacks, they shot his place to pieces. They then pistol-whipped the owner of a drugstore and shot a white civilian who cursed the "damned niggers."

The worst incident occurred in Tampa. On June 6, 1898, white volunteers from Ohio went on a spree. One of them grabbed a two-year-old black child away from his mother. Then, while holding him by the leg, head down, his friends opened fire with their pistols. Their object was not to hit the child, but to see who could put a bullet through the sleeve of his shirt. After a few shots, the winner handed the screaming child back to his mother. As far as they were concerned, they'd had their "fun" and could return to camp. But some black infantry-men disagreed. Upon learning of the shooting, they ran through the streets firing guns, wrecking shops, and beating up whites. Local lawmen dived for cover, and the riot ended only when the troopers' officers stepped in. Commanders hushed up the incident, to keep it from undermining public confidence. After all, the United States had gone to war to free Cuba from oppression, and it would not look right to dramatize oppression at home.

Tampa had been taken over by the military. Early in May, President McKinley appointed an army high command, with Major General Nelson A. Miles as commanding general of the army. A Medal of Honor winner during the Civil War, Miles later took a leading role in the Indian wars. Chief Sitting Bull of the Sioux, Joseph of the Nez Perce, and Geronimo had all been captured by Miles; it was his men who'd carried out the Wounded Knee massacre.

Miles's field commander for the Cuban campaign was Major General William R. Shafter. Six feet tall, with big hands and the lumbering walk of grizzly bear, Shafter looked like two men rolled into one. He weighed over three hundred pounds and had a high-pitched, squeaky voice. "His immense abdomen," an officer wrote home, "hung down, yes, actually hung down between his legs." Yet he was fearless, knew every trick of his trade, and was one of the best marksmen in the army.

The deputy commander was Major General Joseph P. Wheeler. A short, thin man with a white beard, he looked like a mischievous boy decked out in false whiskers and his father's clothes. Yet he was as hard as nails. As "Fightin' Joe" Wheeler, he'd been one of the Confederacy's leading cavalry officers. Famous for his boldness and slapdash tactics, he'd ignored Yankee bullets; friends said he

Overweight and slow moving, Civil War veteran William R. Shafter commanded the American army sent to Cuba in 1898.

Known as "Fighting Joe," General Joseph Wheeler had been one of Robert E. Lee's finest cavalry officers during the Civil War.

never stayed in one place long enough for God to put his finger on him. When the Spanish war began, Wheeler was invited to the White House. As the last Civil War veteran to be president, McKinley saw a chance to erase the last scars of that terrible confict. "There must be a high-ranking officer from the South,"he said. "There must be a symbol that the old days are gone. I need you."

Fightin' Joe agreed to wear the blue Yankee uniform. Years later, after his death, he was buried in that same uniform. Civil War comrades were amazed when his coffin was opened for their last good-bye. "Jesus, General," a veteran stammered. "I hate to think of what old Stonewall's* going to say when he sees you arrivin' in that uniform!"

The generals and their staffs moved into the Tampa Bay Hotel, a huge building that had never housed more than a few dozen tourists at a time. It now swarmed with army officers. Telegraph operators were forever sending messages to, and receiving messages from, Washington. One room sounded like a gunnery range, as typists hammered out reports on their bulky machines. Several officers spent their days planning for the upcoming campaign. Mostly, however, they just renewed old acquaintances. Men who hadn't seen each other in years, who'd fought alongside or against one another in the Civil War, gathered on the shady porches. Sitting in rocking chairs, they talked and drank mint-scented iced tea. At night, under colored lanterns, they danced with the local women. Although impatient to get at the enemy,

*Confederate General Thomas J. ("Stonewall") Jackson was one of the best fighting men America ever produced.

they also enjoyed marking time in these pleasant surroundings. One officer noted, jokingly: "Gentlemen, as General Sherman truly said, 'War is hell.' "

Those in the troop camps saw little to joke about. With the thermometer at 100° in the shade, they sweltered in their woolen uniforms. Yet they were happy to get into the shade, if only for a few minutes; mostly, they were in the sun, marching and shooting on the target range. Coming as they did from different parts of the country, they had to get used to each other's ways. Yankees laughed at the Southerners' drawl. The Southerners took offense, and fists flew until the military police arrived. New Yorkers growled about the steady diet of beans: "Beans for breakfast, beans for lunch, beans for dinner—what t'ell!" Bostonians, sons of the city of the baked bean, complained that they never had enough of their favorite food. Off-duty hours were spent in reading, writing letters home, or curled up "in the sack"—sleeping. Soldiers also gambled, particularly at a dice game introduced by the black troopers. They called it "craps."

General Miles wanted to keep them at Tampa all summer. He knew that apart from the Spaniards, the English were the only foreigners ever to have invaded Cuba. In 1741, Admiral Edward Vernon landed with a powerful force. Vernon, for whom George Washington's Virginia home was named, lost most of his men to yellow fever. Miles didn't want history to repeat itself. Rather than invade immediately, he decided to wait until the end of the yellow fever season in the fall. Then he'd land fifty thousand men near Havana, link up with the guerrillas, and smash the Spaniards. In the meantime, the navy would blockade the Cuban ports and the army would send supplies to the guerrillas. It was a sensible plan and would have saved many lives—had the Spaniards co-operated.

Early in May, Americans learned that a Spanish task force had sailed for the Caribbean under Admiral Pascual Cervera. The task force consisted of four cruisers—*Infanta María Teresa, Almirante Oquendo, Cristóbal Colón, Vizcaya*—two destroyers, and four smaller vessels. Having put to sea, the warships disappeared into the vastness of the Atlantic Ocean.

The yellow press spoke ominously about the "enemy at the gates," and soon their readers were asking questions. Where is Cervera? Will he attack us? Where is the United States Navy?

Americans gave themselves a good scare. They imagined demons lurking everywhere.

The entire East Coast was thrown into a panic. Rumors spread like wildfire. Nothing was too silly to be believed. Someone heard from someone else who knew that Cervera was bound for New York, intending to destroy the Statue of Liberty. No, someone else knew for sure that he was bound for Charleston, South Carolina, a major seaport. Reports of sightings came from places hundreds of miles apart. Maine lobstermen swore that they'd heard gunfire far out at sea. Early risers on the Virginia shore saw "destroyers" outlined against the horizon. Fishermen passed the enemy "task force" in a rain squall; luckily, the Spaniards hadn't seen them or they'd all be in Davy Jones's locker.

Panicky citizens tried to save themselves in any way they could. Boston businessmen moved their valuables to inland banks. Parents planned to evacuate children from coastal areas. Congress was flooded with appeals from governors, mayors, and city councils to rescue their communities before it was too late. One governor even refused to allow the National Guard to leave his state's borders.

The Navy Department was badgered with requests to "do something"—anything. It did what it could to reassure civilians, although, had they known the truth, they would have worried still more. Shore defense guns that hadn't been fired since the Civil War were uncovered and oiled. These were powerful weapons, provided the enemy gave them a clear shot. Merchant ships were fitted with light deck guns and stationed all the way from Maine to the Gulf of Mexico. A cruiser could have sunk any of these slow-moving craft within minutes.

Destroying Cervera became the chief aim of the war. And with good reason, too. His purpose was not to attack the American coast but to break any naval blockade of Cuba. As long as even one harbor remained open to him, the Americans dared not invade the island. If they sailed from Florida, his cruisers might pounce on them at night, drowning thousands of soldiers. Even if they managed to come ashore safely, he could cut them off until Spanish land forces starved them into surrender.

The navy formed two squadrons to deal with Cervera. The first, or "Flying Squadron," was commanded by Rear Admiral Winfield Scott Schley. Its mission was to find Cervera and pin him down until the second squadron arrived. This was the Atlantic Fleet, complete with battleships, under Admiral Sampson. There was no doubt about the winner if the fleets ever traded shots. Barring a miracle, or unbelievable stupidity on the Americans' part, Cervera didn't have a chance. No cruiser could survive alone against the firepower of a battleship.

The Americans dashed around the Caribbean like a pack of hunting dogs. Sampson peeked into Havana Harbor. Cervera wasn't there. Then he swung down to San Juan, Puerto Rico. The Spaniard wasn't there, either, but Sampson lobbed a few thirteen-inch shells into the town as a sort of calling card. Nor did Schley have better luck until he neared Santiago de Cuba on Cuba's southern coast. On May 29, he saw the *Cristóbal Colón* anchored at the harbor's mouth. He would gladly have gone in after Cervera, but the harbor defenses were too strong. El Morro, a fortress bristling with cannon, overlooked the narrow entrance from a high bluff. Powerful batteries guarded the approaches from the shore. Schley could only set up a bockade and call for reinforcements.

Sampson arrived two days later to take charge. He arranged his ships in a half-circle six miles from the harbor entrance and kept their searchlights focused on it at night. In addition, he decided to "plug" the entrance to make sure Cervera stayed put.

Sampson selected Lieutenant Richmond Pearson Hobson for the dangerous assignment. Hobson, a trained naval engineer, and seven volunteers were to turn the coal-carrier *Merrimac* into a steam-powered bomb. Ten torpedoes would be attached to the vessel's port side and connected to electrical batteries. On a dark, moonless night, Hobson was to slip it past El Morro into the narrowest part of the channel. *Merrimac* was 333 feet long and the channel only 350 feet wide at this point. Swinging the vessel crosswise, he'd explode the torpedoes and

Rear Admiral William T. Sampson commanded the American blockading squadron at Santiago de Cuba.

lead his men to safety in the lifeboat. If all went well, the wreck would become a steel plug, blocking the channel and trapping Cervera in the inner harbor.

June 3, 1898. At 2 A.M. *Merrimac* set out on her last voyage. The night was pitch black, except for occasional lightning flashes on the ridge beyond Santiago. The ridge was called San Juan, and soon every American would know its name.

Slowly, quietly, *Merrimac* neared the mouth of the channel. Nothing stirred on shore; she hadn't been seen— yet. But as she passed El Morro, a searchlight beam stabbed the darkness, followed by orange flashes and red balls of flame. She'd come too close to a Spanish patrol boat, whose captain opened fire with his lead squirters.

The shots alerted the shore batteries, which roared into action. Shells tore into the *Merrimac,* but she kept moving. She'd just entered the channel when bullets began striking her with a steady *ping ping ping ping.* Two Spanish infantry regiments, one on either side of the waterway, were blazing away with two thousand Mausers. The vessel was so large, and they were so close, that it was impossible to miss. Hobson and his men lay prone on the deck, praying not to be blown out of the water.

They had reached the narrowest part of the channel. Hobson took a deep breath and shouted to the helmsman: "Hard aport!" But instead of swinging crosswise, *Merrimac* continued toward the inner harbor, straight as an arrow. Her rudder had been shot away and she was out of control.

Hobson was desperate. Turning to a sailor, he ordered him to detonate the torpedoes. A second later there was a roar as two of the torpedoes exploded. The others wouldn't fire because shells had cut their battery connections. With part of her left side blown away, *Merrimac* began taking water, but she refused to turn or slow down. She sped through the channel into the inner harbor, where a Spanish cruiser and destroyer were waiting with torpedoes. These struck below the waterline, stopping her in her tracks and sinking her quickly. She lay inside the harbor, leaving plenty of room for the Spanish warships to move about freely.

Hobson and his men were shaken but unhurt. Their lifeboat had been blown to splinters, but they managed to climb aboard a raft found floating nearby. They lay there exhausted, knowing that they'd have to surrender. Their only concern was that angry Spaniards might shoot them on sight.

At sunrise, they saw a patrol boat bearing down on their raft. Spanish soldiers were standing at the rail and aiming their rifles—at them! But at the last moment, an officer in a white uniform made them hold their fire.

The patrol boat came alongside and deckhands helped

the Americans climb aboard. Hobson, his teeth chattering after a night in the water, stood before the officer. The Spaniard looked at him and smiled. *"Valiente!"* he said in a loud voice. "Brave!" Then he turned and walked away. Only later did the Americans learn that they'd been rescued by Admiral Cervera himself.

Admiral Sampson realized that the blockade would go on for a long time. In order to refuel and repair his ships, he needed a base close to Santiago. Guantanamo Bay forty miles to the east was perfect in every way.

On June 6, the cruiser *Marblehead* and the gunboat *Yankee* appeared off Guantanamo. After a brief bombardment, they destroyed the old fort overlooking the bay and scattered the defenders. Four days later, 650 men of the First Marine Battalion went ashore.

Meeting only light resistance, the marines set up outposts and began to build a camp. The Spaniards, however,

Admiral Pasual Cervera, head of the Spanish Fleet in Cuba, admired bravery on either side.

had only been driven off, not defeated. One evening, while most of the marines were enjoying a swim in the bay, they struck. Surprise was total, at least for the moment. Leathernecks, naked as newborns, grabbed their rifles and returned fire. Marine counterattacks later overran a key hill position, forcing the enemy inland and out of striking range.

Stephen Crane, a famous reporter, was with the marines. Three years before, he'd written *The Red Badge of Courage,* which immediately became a classic story of the Civil War. Crane was an unlikely person to write a war novel. The book had come strictly from his imagination, since he'd never heard a shot fired in anger, much less seen a person killed. Guantanamo changed all that.

In the first days after the landing, Crane had become friendly with a young doctor named John Blair Gibbs. The two were going about their own business when the Spaniards attacked. Crane dove for cover. He lay on the sand, feeling the hot wind of the bullets inches above his head. Nearby he could hear a man dying.

I heard someone dying near me. He was dying hard. Hard. It took him a long time to die. He breathed as all noble machinery breathes when it is making its gallant strike against breaking, breaking. But he was going to break. . . . Every wave, vibration, of his anguish beat against my senses. He was long past groaning. There was only the bitter strife for air which pulsed out into the night in a clear penetrating whistle with intervals of terrible silence in which I held my own breath. . . . I thought this man would never die. I wanted him to die. Ultimately he died. At the moment [an officer] came bustling along erect amid the spitting bullets. I knew him by his voice. 'Where's the doctor?

There's some wounded men over there. Where's the doctor?" A
man answered briskly: 'Just died this minute, sir!' It was as if
he had said: 'Just gone around the corner this minute, sir.'

Crane admitted that the shock of Gibbs' death made him
grow up—fast.

Many American boys would soon grow up in the same
way.

Although the navy had trapped Cervera, it couldn't
make him surrender. As long as he remained in the harbor, behind El Morro and the shore batteries, he was safe.
The Americans had no choice: they must take Santiago
from the land, not the sea.

On June 6, as black troopers rioted in Tampa and warships bombarded Guantanamo, Shafter received orders to
sail for Cuba. That's when his troubles really began, for,
despite weeks of planning, his inexperienced staff seemed
unable to do anything right. The result was a gigantic
foul-up that nearly wrecked the expedition before it
sailed.

Shafter's supply system was a shambles. A light railroad connected Tampa City to Port Tampa ten miles
away. Built for local traffic, it was unable to handle the
flood of supplies that poured in from every part of
the country. Hundreds of freight cars were stalled along
the tracks and at spurs off the main line. These cars were
filled with supplies, only no one knew what they contained. There were no packing lists, and supply officers
had to break into each car to learn its contents.

Food supplies, particularly fresh meat, rotted in the
heat. Canned beef, however, looked as if it would last

forever. Beef came in bright red cans stamped with the date 1894. To keep it from spoiling, the packer had sprinkled it with a chemical preservative. The chemical was so strong, and the meat so disgusting in taste and appearance, that soldiers called it "embalmed beef."

Those in charge of loading the transports didn't know the first thing about their job. Food and equipment were tossed aboard carelessly, without a thought for what the troops would need most when they landed. Thus, some ships had hardtack for the men but no shells for their field guns. Field guns were buried deep in the holds rather than kept handy to support the troops ashore. Sixty cannon were simply left behind. They would be sorely missed.

Troop transportation was even worse. Planners had miscalculated the number of men the ships could carry. There was room for about sixteen thousand men rather than the originally planned twenty-seven thousand. Entire regiments would have to stay behind. The cavalry would have to fight on foot, since there was space only for officers' mounts.

This came as a shock to the troops. They'd set their hearts on going to Cuba. Many had given up good civilian jobs to serve their country, only to be left behind at the last moment. Officers and men were tremendously disappointed on hearing the bad news. Others, however, were thankful that they'd been chosen. "We should be glad to go on all fours rather than not at all," Roosevelt wrote to a friend.

The lucky regiments had to move from camp to dockside on their own. Although trains had been assigned to each, they never arrived on time, if they came at all. It was hit or miss. For example, the black troopers of the Tenth

Doughboys board a ship at Tampa Bay, Florida, for the voyage to Cuba. It was a sweltering hot day, which their woolen uniforms didn't make any cooler.

Cavalry traveled in luxury: they had fancy coaches with ice in the water coolers. Unfortunately, they had no food. When they arrived at the docks, an officer tried to buy them food at a lunch counter, only to be told that serving "colored men" would be bad for business. The Sixth Infantry, however, had plenty of food, only the troops had to travel in cattle cars. That's when they learned the meaning of the army saying, "Hurry up and wait!" For hours men stood up to their ankles in soft manure until permission came to move forward. Upon reaching the docks, they had to sit for more hours waiting under the broiling sun.

Not the Rough Riders. Orders came for them to march to one place, then to another, only to see trains pass them without stopping. But Theodore Roosevelt was not a patient man. He stood in the middle of the track and flagged down the next train, an engine pulling a string of empty coal cars. Ignoring the driver's protests, he had his men climb aboard with all their equipment.

T.R.'s buckaroos meant to reach Cuba or die trying. As the train chugged along, they chanted:

> *Rough, tough, we're the stuff;*
> *We want to fight, and we can't get enough!*

Confusion reigned at the docks. No one knew what ship they'd been assigned. All they could see were thousands of men milling about, searching for a vessel to board.

Once again luck favored the Rough Riders. Seeing the ship *Yucatán* anchored offshore, Colonel Wood jumped into a steam launch and hijacked it.

In the meantime, T.R. had lined the men up at dockside. They were tired, hungry, and covered with coal dust. The ship seemed like heaven. As it pulled alongside the dock, they swarmed aboard. Moments later, another regiment came along to claim her.

"Hello," said T.R., "what can I do for you?"

"That's *our* ship," a captain protested.

"Do tell," T.R. replied, flashing his best Toothadore smile. "Well, we seem to have it, don't we?"

Then, for good measure, the Rough Riders jeered and threw lumps of coal from the *Yucatán*'s bunkers.

Next morning, as the transports made ready to sail, Shafter received a telegram from the War Department. Patrol boats had seen two Spanish "cruisers" prowling offshore. The expedition must wait until they were located and destroyed.

Whatever the patrol boats saw, it wasn't enemy cruisers. But while the navy searched, the army suffered aboard the hot, overcrowded transports. Finally, on the evening of June 14, the all-clear signal was flashed.

Thirty-two transports blew their whistles, weighed anchor, and began to move. They carried the largest military force that had ever left American shores: 819 officers, 15,058 troops, 30 civilian clerks, 107 dock workers, 272 mule skinners, 2,295 horses and mules.

Once clear of the harbor, the transports were joined by fourteen warships. As the shore faded in the distance, they formed three columns and steamed southward under a canopy of stars.

IV
The Cuban Campaign

"All men who feel any power of joy in battle know what it is like when the wolf rises in the heart."
— *Theodore Roosevelt*

The invasion fleet sailed along the southern coast of Cuba. Life aboard the transports was miserable, like being in a heated sewer. Troops, dirty and soaked with sweat, slept in bunks three levels high with two men to a bunk. It was so crowded that many left the stifling holds and went topside to sleep on the wooden deck. Personal cleanliness was impossible, except for officers, who had their own washrooms. On the *Miami,* for example, there were twelve toilets for twelve hundred men. There was no water for washing and practically none for drinking. Richard Harding Davis, the most famous war correspondent of the day, said that ship's water "smelled like a frog pond or a stable-yard, and it tasted as it smelt."

On June 20, its sixth day at sea, the fleet anchored near Santiago. General Shafter and Admiral Sampson went ashore to meet with General Calixto García, the local

Soldiers aboard the invasion fleet bound for Cuba lived in hot, cramped, stuffy quarters that stank of damp and human sweat.

rebel commander. García, who knew the countryside like the back of his hand, suggested landing at two points on the coast: Daiquirí and Siboney. Daiquirí was a tiny village with a rickety pier sixteen miles east of Santiago. Siboney, five miles nearer the target, was merely a stretch of beach with a row of native huts. Both places, said García, were poorly defended and the landings should go smoothly. Since the Americans had no plans of their own, they accepted the Cuban's strategy with little discussion.

Everyone was glad when the order to land finally came. Anything, including Spanish bullets, was better than the transports. For the next day and a half, they prepared for the big event. Enlisted men oiled rifles and sharpened bayonets one more time. Personal things were wrapped in "horse collars," blanket rolls tied at each end and slung across the shoulders. On some ships, they gave the traditional cry: "To the officers—may they get killed, wounded, or promoted." It was like actors saying "Break a leg!" at the opening of a new show. The officers smiled (sort of) and wished each other good luck. T.R. grinned from ear to ear, waved his hat in the air, and stomped about in his own version of an Indian war dance.

Dawn, June 22.

American warships steamed parallel to the shore and opened fire. Although not a Spaniard was to be seen, the navy wasn't taking any chances. Daiquirí and the hills beyond were pounded with high-explosive shells. After a half-hour the guns fell silent, clearing the way for the assault force.

Meantime, troops were scrambling over the sides of their transports into the waiting longboats. Like bucking broncos, the longboats bounced and rolled in the waves. For the nervous troopers, timing was everything. If you jumped to soon, you crashed when the boat lurched upward. If you waited too long, you fell many feet as it dropped into the trough between two waves.

When they were fully loaded, several boats were roped together in line and towed by a navy steam launch. The journey was wet and bumpy. The wind-tossed spray soaked the troopers to the skin. The constant up-down motion made them seasick. Many leaned over the side to vomit or, moving too slowly, vomited over themselves and their neighbors.

The lead boats came alongside the pier, followed by others that sped through the surf onto the beach itself. Those at the pier had a rough time because it was built some fifteen feet above the water. In order to land, men had to wait for a wave to raise their boat level with the pier, then leap across. To miss your timing meant death; the weight of your boots, horse collar, and ammunition belt would drag you under. Two black cavalrymen drowned in this way.

Horses and mules were pushed overboard to find their own way ashore. Many of the animals were so confused after being in the ships' dark holds that they panicked

Troops landing on the dock at Daiquiri, Cuba. The water was so rough that some men fell overboard and were crushed when their boats slammed against the dock.

when they hit the water. Some swam out to sea and drowned, while others were swept along by the current and crushed against rocks. One group was saved by a quick-thinking bugler; he blew "right turn" and the horses, true to their training, turned toward the shore.

When Fightin' Joe Wheeler landed, he sent four Rough Riders to raise the flag over an abandoned hilltop fort. As Old Glory unfurled against the sky, the men celebrated as if they'd already won the war. Soldiers waved their hats and fired their rifles into the air. Ships' whistles began tooting, joined by musicians' drum rolls and bugle calls. The uproar lasted fifteen minutes, then stopped as a band aboard the transport *Matteawan* struck up "The Star-Spangled Banner." Soldiers and sailors stood at attention while the band played, then gave three cheers that could be heard for miles.

Only then did the doughboys realize what had happened. They stood on the beach, staring at the brush-covered hillsides. Not a Spaniard had been seen, not a shot fired at them. For some unknown reason, the Spaniards had simply run away when the naval bombardment began. Had the Spaniards dug in and waited it out, as the Japanese would do at places like Iwo Jima in World War II, the Americans could have been slaughtered at the water's edge.

Next morning, Wheeler marched to Siboney to join the rest of the army. His men were busy making camp when he received some bad news. Scouts reported that the Spaniards held a gap in the hills to the north. The place was called Las Guásimas, after the guásima trees that grew there—low trees whose nuts are used for pig feed. The Americans had to pass through Las Guásimas on their to way Santiago. If the Spaniards held onto it, the Americans would be pinned to the coast until the yellow fever season began. They'd then have to leave Cuba or lose their army without ever fighting a battle. General Shafter was still aboard ship, so Fightin' Joe ordered an attack before the Spaniards could strengthen their position.

On June 24, Wheeler led a strike force up the trail to Las Guásimas. When the trail forked, he took the First and Tenth Cavalry to the right, while the Rough Riders went to the left. His plan was to close in on the Spaniards from both sides, trapping them between the two columns.

Although the men knew that the enemy was hiding up ahead, they didn't know exactly where. That didn't bother the Rough Riders. They were in high spirits and couldn't keep their mouths shut. As they marched along the narrow jungle trail, they joked, laughed, and argued at the tops of their voices.

Wood and T.R. were at the head of the column when they found the body of a guerrilla sprawled across the path. "There's a Spanish outpost just ahead," said Wood, sensing danger, "and the men must stop talking."

The order was passed down the line. But instead of whispering it, sergeants bellowed as if they were on a parade ground. "Stop talking', can't ye?" one cried. "Ah, say, can't ye stop talkin'?" shouted another.

Those were the last words some Rough Riders ever heard. Suddenly the air vibrated with sound. There was a shrill *z-z-z-z-z-eu* overhead, followed by a sharp *crack*. Mausers!

The hidden Spaniards opened fire and Americans began to drop. The enemy position was invisible, thanks to dense jungle and smokeless powder. Unable to see their attackers, the Rough Riders dived for cover. Wood was calm under the hail of bullets, but T.R. was so excited that he jumped up and down. Never mind the bullets, this was "bully!" The bullets missed him, although one hit a tree inches from his head, filling his eyes and ears with splinters. Those first shots, he explained later, triggered something deep inside of him. It was the joy of battle, the spirit of the wolf rising in his heart.

The Rough Riders were pinned down. It was frustrating, maddening, to be shot at by those they couldn't see. Whenever they raised their heads, the Spaniards let loose a volley. Anyone foolish enough to be standing was bowled over by the Mauser bullets. The Mauser packed a terrific punch. The force of a bullet striking an outstretched arm, for example, was enough to spin a man around before he crumpled to the ground. You knew when a fellow was hit nearby, for a Mauser bullet always made a loud *chug* when it struck flesh.

Richard Harding Davis saved the day at Las Guásimas. Crawling to T.R.'s side, he trained his binoculars on a pile of vine-covered rocks. "There they are colonel!" he said, grabbing Roosevelt's arm. "Look over there! You can see their hats!" Sure enough, scores of Spanish sombreros were visible only a hundred yards away.

T.R. ordered his best marksmen to return fire. Slowly, gently, they squeezed their triggers. Each time a Krag barked, a Spaniard slumped over or leaped up, screaming in pain. That did it. Once they'd identified the enemy position, all the Rough Riders opened fire. Davis joined in with a rifle he'd found lying on the ground.

By now, however, Wheeler's cavalrymen had gone into

action on the right. Cavalrymen and Rough Riders began to press the enemy's flanks. Small groups of men would run forward, then drop to the ground or duck behind trees. Running and firing, they'd take turns covering one another, until they could see the Spaniards' faces. Startled by such recklessness, the Spaniards broke from cover and ran down the trail toward Santiago.

Fightin' Joe could no longer contain himself. As they fled, he gave the Rebel yell and shouted, "We've got the damn Yankees on the run!" The Civil War was never far from his mind.

Although they'd outnumbered the Americans by five hundred men, the Spaniards retreated. Those fellows, they muttered, were *"muy loco,"* very crazy. Wildmen, they ignored all the rules of warfare. "When we fired a volley," a Spanish prisoner said, "instead of falling back they came forward. That is not the way to fight, to come closer at every volley." Worse, "they tried to catch us with their hands!"

The trail was now open, allowing the Americans to come within sight of Santiago. Still, it was rough going. Despite the engineers' efforts, the trail could not handle the wagon and mule trains hauling supplies from Siboney. It was so narrow in places that hours were wasted in untangling traffic jams. Rations, when they arrived, were both nasty and scarce. Soldiers were forced to eat embalmed beef and beans soaked in hog fat; when opened, the cans smelled like garbage pails in the damp heat. But the lack of tobacco was felt most keenly. Tobacco was the doughboy's all-purpose drug. With a pipe (cigarettes hadn't become popular yet), he could steady

A mule train bringing ammunition to the front at San Juan Hill.

his nerves, drive away hunger, and bear aches and pains. Those who couldn't get tobacco smoked a mixture of dried grass and roots. Really desperate men filled their pipes with dried horse manure.

Nights were anything but restful. Doughboys would lie on the damp ground, trying to fall asleep. When they finally dozed off, they'd be jolted awake.

"Halt! Who goes there?" a sentry would cry as he fired into the darkness. One shot inspired others, and within seconds all the sentries were blazing away. The enemy was near, they'd shout. They could could hear him prowling in the jungle.

The "enemy," it turned out, wasn't Spaniards, but land crabs, ugly creatures that moved about noisily in search of food. Not only did they scare the sentries, they tormented the sleeping men. Soldiers constantly awoke to find crabs crawling over their bodies, clinging to their ears, and biting their noses. Red ants, their bites as painful as electric needles, brought their own special form of misery.

The doughboys had reason to be jittery. From their camp, they could could see the enemy defenses three miles away. The Spaniards' main defense line ran along the crest of San Juan Ridge. Its key positions, however, were the trenches and barbed wire fences on San Juan Hill and Kettle Hill. These were supported by the village of El Caney two-and-a-half miles to the northeast. In addition to barbed wire and trenches, El Caney's defenders had built a small fort and cut loopholes in the walls of a stone church; Hernán Cortés is said to have prayed in the church before setting out on the conquest of Mexico. Although only 1,041 Spaniards manned the defenses, they were in strong positions.

Shafter planned to begin his assault on El Caney. After a brief bombardment, he'd send fifty-four hundred men to overwhelm the defenders by sheer weight of numbers. That, he believed, shouldn't take more than an hour. With El Caney secure, he'd hurl his main force, ten thousand men, against San Juan Hill. Once they stormed the Spanish positions, Santiago would lay helpless beneath them. The city would have to surrender, along with Cervera's ships, thus ending the war.

Shafter's plan, however, was risky and poorly thought out. Before attacking the two hills, his men would have to march down the jungle trail. But the trail was not only narrow, it had thick bushes on either side, making it impossible for the troops to spread out. Every Spanish rifle was zeroed in on the trail; although the riflemen couldn't see through the jungle canopy, they could fire blindly and have a good chance of hitting someone. The trail opened onto a meadow in front of and below the San Juan trenches. Americans who reached the meadow would have no cover except clumps of waist-high grass. The Spaniards could pick them off like sitting ducks, especially since the Americans had little artillery support. Only sixteen small field guns were available for the attack; the heavy guns loaded at Tampa were still buried in the holds of the transports. For some reason Shafter didn't ask for the navy's help. Its rifles could easily have shelled the ridge and the Spanish trenches. Perhaps he wanted the army to take all the credit for capturing Santiago.

Shafter's aides saw the problem and suggested a way to solve it. Troops could cut other trails, each ending at the meadow. Thus, when the time came, the whole army could charge the hills at once. But the overweight general wasn't his normal self. The Cuban heat so tortured him that he couldn't think straight. He was so miserable, so exhausted, that he brushed aside their advice. He then lay down on his cot, where he spent most of the next two months. Not once did he see the battle that followed, or try to direct it.

July 1, 1898. The Americans began to move toward El Caney before dawn. Unlike the main trail to the San Juan hills, El Caney could be reached by a side trail shielded from the Spanish riflemen.

The marching troops were surprised to see a horseman in a black business suit watching them as they set out.

"Hi, there, Willie!" some New Yorkers called, recognizing him.

Others took up the cry, and before long "Hi, there, Willie!" was being shouted from one end of the column to the other.

William Randolph Hearst had come to see the war in person. It was his war, something he'd created, and he was proud of it. "How Do You Like the *Journal*'s War?" he'd asked in one headline. But he wasn't boastful this morning. Perhaps he was squeamish, now that young men were about to die in "his" war. "Good luck!" he called. "Good luck be with you, my boys!"

The fight for El Caney began with a shelling from four American cannon, followed by an all-out infantry attack. This time the Spaniards held their ground with determination. Three times the Americans charged, only to be thrown back with heavy losses. After an hour's fighting, it became clear that the village's defenders were tougher than Shafter had imagined. The battle raged until the late afternoon, long after the fall of San Juan Ridge. The doughboys were able to break through only after El Caney's Spanish commander was killed and his men began running out of ammunition.

At the same time, the main advance on San Juan Hill had gotten underway. Ten thousand men crowded the jungle trail, all heading in the same direction. The Spaniards were waiting for them. As they came forward, the air vibrated with the screech of Mauser bullets. Even veterans became tense. Brave men felt a tightness in the throat, their mouths went dry, and their stomach seemed tied up in knots.

Soon they were surrounded by horrible sights and sounds. The wounded littered the ground, writhing and screaming. Comrades, eager to help, had been ordered to keep going, since any pause would slow up the march. The dead, of course, needed no one's help. Private Charles Post of the Seventy-First Infantry saw his first corpse that morning. A lieutenant lay beside the trail. "His glazed eyes were staring at the trees overhead, and the ants were already crawling over his eyeballs," Post recalled.

An army major stood over the body, crying hysterically and calling to the passing troops.

"Cover him, somebody. Dammit, he's an officer! Cover him up!'

"Cover him up yourself!" someone answered. They had better things to do than bother about a "stiff."

A signal corps observation balloon made things even worse. The balloon, a giant gas-filled bag with two officers in a basket dangling underneath, was towed by men on the ground. The balloon marked the position of the regiments crowding the trail below for the Spanish artillery. Shells exploded, showering them with steel splinters. One black trooper said each shell sang as it approached: "I want ye! I want ye!"

Doughboys cursed the balloon and the idiots who'd taken it aloft. But their curses turned to cheers when a splinter tore the bag and sent it crashing to earth. The balloonists, however, survived to tell what they'd seen. Their report: Spaniards were firing on the trail from San Juan Hill!

By now troops were exiting the trail and moving off to the right. Since they had no orders to go further, they could only keep low in the grass and wait. The open

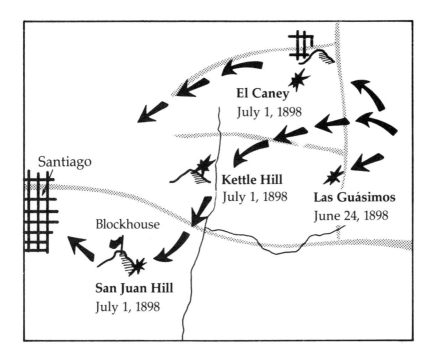

Santiago

El Caney
July 1, 1898

Kettle Hill
July 1, 1898

Las Guásimos
June 24, 1898

Blockhouse

San Juan Hill
July 1, 1898

meadow stretched before them. Above them were the Spanish trenches. Dead and wounded doughboys lay in the grass, which had become flecked with blood.

The Rough Riders crouched at the foot of Kettle Hill— that is, everyone but Captain William "Bucky" O'Neill, the former sheriff of Prescott, Arizona. O'Neill believed that an officer should never take cover, since that might weaken his men's fighting spirit. He stood in the open, calmly smoking a cigarette while bullets whipped overhead.

"Better lie down, sir," a sergeant warned.

Bucky laughed and blew a cloud of smoke. "Sergeant," he said, looking down, "the Spanish bullet hasn't been made that can kill me!" But he was wrong. At that instant one struck him in the mouth and came out the back of his head. He was dead before he hit the ground.

The troops felt helpless and angry at the same time. Here they were, pinned down and unable to retreat, for the trail behind them was jammed with men. Nor could they stay put, for that meant certain death; sooner or later, they were bound to be shot from above. There was only one thing to do—get the enemy before he got them. And that meant storming the two hills.

Yet they were paralyzed without orders. The army's chain of command had broken down. Unit leaders—lieutenants and captains—hadn't been told what to do in this particular situation. Field commanders—colonels and generals—hadn't the authority to launch a general assault. Only Shafter could do that, and he lay moaning on his cot three miles behind the lines.

Just when things seemed worst, a new sound rose above the din of battle. Puzzled doughboys looked at each other anxiously, then smiled as they recognized the sound. A detachment of three Gatling guns had gone into action. The Gatling was an early version of the machine gun. Nicknamed the "coffee grinder," because it used a hand crank instead of a trigger, it could fire nine hundred bullets a minute. Those bullets were now spraying the San Juan trenches, forcing the Spanish riflemen to keep their heads down.

The Gatlings turned the tide of battle. Without waiting for orders, soldiers took matters into their own hands. It began with Lieutenant Jules Ord of the Sixth Infantry. Ord, the son of a Civil War hero, was fed up with hugging the ground. As the enemy's fire slackened, he stood up, tore off his shirt, and tossed it away. "Now I'm ready for

Nicknamed the "coffee grinder," the Gatling gun was an early version of the machine gun. Guns such as this turned the tide during the attack on San Juan Hill.

anything," he cried. "Good-bye, if I don't come back!"

Holding a pistol in one hand and a bayonet in the other, Ord turned to the men crouched in the grass around him. "Come on! Come on, you men! We can't stay here! Follow me!"

And follow him they did. Yelling like lunatics, fifty doughboys broke cover and raced toward San Juan Hill. Ord reached the hill first, only to be shot dead. But the others kept going. Come hell or high water, they meant to get to the top.

What followed was not an organized battle. There were no cavalry charges, no battle flags fluttering in the breeze, no infantry columns advancing behind glinting bayonets. It was a "soldiers' battle" all the way.

As Ord raced across the meadow, a contagious frenzy seized the onlookers. Sergeants sprang to their feet, shouting: "Get the Garlics! Charge!" Buglers sounded the charge, then grabbed rifles and joined the rush. Officers had no choice but to follow their men or be left behind.

The doughboys came on by tens, by fifties, by hundreds. Cursing their way through the tall grass, falling and picking themselves up, they climbed the slope with their rifles pressed across their chests. Barbed wire fences barred the way, but they smashed the posts with rifle butts. Richard Harding Davis could scarcely believe his eyes. He'd seen other charges in other wars, but nothing like this. "It was much more wonderful than any swinging charge could have been," he wrote. "They walked to greet death at every step, many of them, as they advanced, sinking suddenly or pitching forward . . . but others waded on, stubbornly, forming a thin blue line that kept

Without orders, Lieutenant Jules G. Ord began the charge up San Juan Hill. Although he was shot dead moments later, others, following his example, began a mass movement toward the enemy trenches.

creeping higher and higher up the hill. It was as inevitable as the rising tide. It was a miracle of self-sacrifice, a triumph of bull-dog courage, which one watched breathless with wonder."

Again Theodore Roosevelt felt the wolf rising in his heart. Since Colonel Wood had been temporarily assigned to another unit, he commanded the Rough Riders at Kettle Hill. Sitting atop Little Texas, he was a perfect target as he rode from one group of men to another. Bullets whined close to his ears, but he never flinched. His only fear was losing his eyeglasses, since he was nearly blind without them. To avoid this calamity, he had four extra pairs clipped to his uniform and one pair sewn inside his hat. With his precious eyeglasses secure, he was ready for anything.

No Rough Rider wanted action more than the Colonel. When the attack on San Juan Hill began, Roosevelt had the bugler sound the charge. All but one man stood up and moved forward. T.R. saw him cowering behind a bush and ordered him to his feet. The man, paralyzed with fear, wouldn't move. "Are you afraid to stand when I am on horseback?" T.R. roared. Just then the man stiffened and pitched forward. A bullet, aimed at Roosevelt, had missed him and drilled the man lengthwise from head to foot.

The Rough Riders rushed the slope, joined by black troopers from the Ninth and Tenth Cavalry. Except for T.R., they were all on foot. He galloped ahead of everyone, armed only with a pistol salvaged from the wreck of the *Maine*. He dismounted at a barbed wire fence just as a Spanish officer appeared. Roosevelt dropped him with one shot.

The cavalrymen broke through the fence and rushed the Spanish trenches. After a short, sharp fight, the enemy fled down the other side of Kettle Hill. The only Spaniards left were the dead sprawled in pools of their own blood. Another man might have been sickened at the sight, but T.R. was thrilled. Trooper Bob Ferguson, a close friend, wrote Mrs. Roosevelt* after the battle: "No hunting trip so far has ever equaled it in Theodore's eyes. . . . When I caught him up the day of the charge . . . [he] was revelling in victory and gore. He had just doubled up a Spanish officer like a 'jack-rabbit' . . . and he encouraged us to look at those 'damned Spanish dead.' "

*After losing his first wife, T.R. married Edith Kermit Carow. They had five children: Theodore, Jr., Kermit, Ethel, Archibald, and Quentin. Theodore, Jr., followed in his father's footsteps. He joined the army, rose to the rank of general, and led a division during the invasion of France in 1944. There was also a daughter, Alice, from Roosevelt's first marriage.

The charge up San Juan Hill as seen by artist William J. Glackens.

A victory portrait. Colonel Theodore Roosevelt and his Rough Riders pose on the crest of San Juan Hill overlooking the city of Santiago.

The doughboys had driven the Spaniards off San Juan Hill. The Stars and Stripes immediately rose above the captured trenches. Men, panting and sweating, sat on the ground and looked back at the way they'd come. "Well, hell, here we are!" said an exhausted trooper.

The battle for San Juan Ridge was over. It had cost 205 American and 215 Spanish lives. The Americans also had 1,180 wounded, the Spaniards 376.

For the wounded, however, the battle had only just begun. Unlike today's soldier, who carries his own first aid kit of bandages, painkillers and antibiotics, the doughboy had only one small bandage and one large one, which could be used as an arm sling. The Spaniards were treated in the hospitals of Santiago, but the American wounded had to go to a field hospital just behind the lines. The "walking wounded" were lucky—they moved by themselves. Seriously wounded men were put into supply wagons used as ambulances. Every bump of the uneven ground was agony, as the wounded bounced up and down on the rough floorboards. Some fellows begged to be put out and allowed to die peacefully under the trees.

The field hospital was staffed by five surgeons. Although able men, they had none of the lifesaving methods we take for granted. There were no X rays to pinpoint an internal injury; to locate a bullet, it was necessary to probe for it with a steel instrument, a painful process that caused dangerous bleeding. Blood transfusions were unknown. Nor were painkillers used for ordinary wounds; only the most seriously wounded men were allowed morphine, a narcotic made from the opium poppy. Ether was used to put patients to sleep during operations.

The surgeons were unprepared for the hundreds of men that needed their help. Their hospital consisted of three large tents with operating tables, a large tent for wounded officers, and six small tents that held a hundred men at most. Basic supplies were totally lacking. There were no cots, mattresses, pillows, or rubber sheets to keep the ground dampness away from the wounded. Except for two or three dozen shirts, there was no hospital clothing. And there was no special food for the sick, only a few jars of beef extract and malted milk, which a surgeon had bought in Tampa with his own money.

As the wounded arrived, they were put on the grass in front of the operating tents. It was a brutally hot day, and they lay in the sun, without shelter, waiting their turn.

Wounded Spanish soldiers wait to be taken to the rear after their capture on San Juan Hill.

An ambulance takes American wounded to a field hospital during the battle for San Juan Hill. The journey in these springless wagons shook the wounded up so badly that many begged to be left to die at the roadside.

American military hospitals in Cuba were crude affairs indeed. Here the wounded rest on cots under canvas, which did little to keep out the tropical heat, dust, and insects.

On the day of the battle, surgeons worked twenty-one hours without a break. Since there were no lanterns, at night they moved the operating tables out of the tents and operated by moonlight or by candles held by orderlies. That was dangerous, because Spanish snipers lurked in the jungle. Not only did they shoot healthy soldiers, they fired into ambulances and at the wounded. Outlined as he was against the moon, a surgeon never knew when a bullet would slam into his back. Fortunately, none were hit.

George Kennan of the American Red Cross described what happened to the patients after their operations:

The tents set apart for wounded soldiers were already full to overflowing, and all that a [stretcher team] could do with a man when they lifted him from the operating table [that] night was to carry him away and lay him down, half-naked as he was, on the water-soaked ground under the stars. Weak and shaken from agony under the surgeon's knife and probe, there he had to lie in the high, wet grass, with no one to look after him, no one to give him food and water if he needed them, no blanket over him, and no pillow under his head. . . . When the sun rose [next] morning, the sufferings of the wounded . . . were intensified rather than relieved, because with sunshine came intense heat, thirst, and surgical fever. . . . The suffering men in the grass [were left] to the care of the camp cooks and a few slightly wounded soldiers, who, although in pain themselves, could still hobble about carrying hard bread and water to their completely disabled and gasping comrades. . . . As one of the army surgeons said to me, with tears very near his eyes: "When I look at those fellows and see what they stand, I am proud of being an American. . . . The world has nothing finer.'

The surgeons were helped by their patients' courage. Refusing to give in to pain, they gritted their teeth and bore it without complaint. "Cheez," murmured a doughboy just off the operating table, "they stuck a rag in one side of me and pulled it out the other side! That's something, ain't it?" A comrade, weakened by loss of blood, looked up at the surgeons and said: "Ah, youse can't kill me. I'm a New Yorker, by God! Youse can't kill me!" One youngster overheard a surgeon say that he didn't expect him to live. "You're a damn liar," he snapped. "I ain't gonna die." Nor did he. Indeed, most of the wounded survived, thanks to the surgeons' use of antiseptic methods. Unlike the old days, when no one knew that germs caused disease, surgeons now washed their hands and sterilized their instruments before operating. These were simple precautions, but they saved countless lives.

The military situation, however, promised even more casualties in the days that followed. San Juan Ridge was only Santiago's *first* line of defense. Behind it, stretching for two miles to the city walls, was a maze of trenches,

American trenches atop San Juan Hill. The building was a Spanish fort, taken after bloody fighting.

barbed wire entanglements, and stone forts.

The enemy seemed as strong as ever, while the Americans felt themselves growing weaker by the hour. Life on the Ridge was an ordeal. Doughboys huddled in trenches reeking of death, garbage, and excrement. By day, the sun beat down like a blowtorch. Men developed painful sunburns, and the glare gave them splitting headaches. Anyone who stood up drew a storm of Mauser bullets; the only way to move about was to crawl on your hands and knees. At night it rained, but since there was no change of clothes, you remained soaked to the skin. Some men "funked"; that is, had nervous breakdowns. Unable to bear the strain, they'd sit motionless for hours or sob uncontrollably until taken to the rear. Their comrades knew that they weren't being cowardly. Like the men on the operating tables, they'd been wounded, only their wounds didn't bleed.

Things looked so bad that Shafter thought of retreating until reinforcements arrived from home. His officers, however, wouldn't hear of the scheme. Not only was it cowardly, it served no useful purpose. They agreed with Fightin' Joe Wheeler, who said that if they retreated, they'd only have to fight again for the same ground. Even with reinforcements, that would mean more heavy losses. Shafter fumbled for a whole day, unable to make up his mind. Then help came from an unexpected source.

The Spanish fleet sailed to its destruction.

General Ramón Blanco, governor of Cuba, was grim when the news came from Santiago. He was in Havana, far from the action, and had no idea of how badly the

Keep your head down! American officers observe enemy positions from the trenches before Santiago. The Spaniards were good marksmen, and more than one careless doughboy felt the sting of their bullets.

American soldiers, wearing their "horse collar" blankets, in action near Santiago.

Americans were hurt. All he knew was that the loss of San Juan Ridge made Santiago's fall inevitable. It was only a matter of time before its food ran out, or the *yanquis* (Yankees) brought heavy guns to blast it to rubble. Nothing could save the proud city.

This raised the question of the fleet trapped in Santiago harbor. If it remained there, the outcome was certain: it would be lost. Either the enemy would capture it, or Admiral Cervera would scuttle it to keep it from falling into their hands. But if it sailed, it might still have a chance. At least a few vessels might break through the blockade. Even if they didn't they might take some of the enemy with them when they sank. Finally, Blanco sent a telegram to Cervera. It was brief and to the point: Leave Santiago immediately.

On the morning of July 3, American lookouts saw the Spanish fleet slip out of the harbor. Six vessels—four cruisers and two destroyers—emerged proudly, gracefully, as if on review. They'd recently been painted and their black hulls, tipped with golden figureheads, glistened in the sunlight. Huge silken banners of red and gold fluttered at the tops of their masts. As they passed beneath the guns of El Morro, one of Cervera's aides shook his head and sighed, "Poor Spain." The fleet, he knew, was no match for the waiting Americans.

Admiral Sampson had gone away for the day with the cruiser *New York,* leaving Admiral Schley in command. All five of the Navy's battleships—*Iowa, Indiana, Massachusetts, Oregon, Texas*—stood offshore with loaded rifles. They were joined by Schley's own flagship, the cruiser *Brooklyn,* and two smaller vessels known as armed yachts. Like

Rear Admiral Winfield Scott Schley defeated the Spanish fleet as it sailed out of Santiago harbor.

Admiral Dewey's men at Manila Bay, his crews would not be satisfied with just a victory. They wanted to annihilate the enemy fleet.

The naval battle of Santiago began with a near-accident that could have spelled disaster for the Americans. As the Spaniards approached, Schley gave the signal to fire. The big guns roared, filling the air with black-powder smoke. Warships, their funnels belching coal smoke, raced after the enemy. Before long, a cloud of smoke shrouded some of the American vessels. It became so thick that at times deckhands could hardly see their hands in front of their faces.

Brooklyn was moving at top speed when a breeze suddenly parted the smoke. There, ahead of her on a collision course, loomed the *Texas.* "Look out for the *Texas,* sir!" the navigator shouted to Schley. "Damn the *Texas!*" the admiral snapped. "Let her look out for herself!" Which is exactly what she did. A quick order threw her engines into reverse, slowing her just as *Brooklyn* roared past. From then on, the battle went without a hitch.

The Spaniards fought bravely, desperately, but in vain. *Maria Teresa,* Cervera's flagship, became the first victim. Shells from *Brooklyn* and *Iowa* exploded piles of ammunition stored belowdecks. Steam pipes burst, sending jets of live steam hissing along the decks; anyone caught in the steam was literally boiled alive. His cruiser a flaming hulk, Cervera ordered her run into the shallows to allow her crew to escape. The last man to leave was the admiral himself. Stripping off his uniform, he crossed himself and went over the side stark naked.

The cruiser *Vizcaya* was next. Pounded by heavy shells, she burst into flame from end to end. The fires burned fiercely, turning her steel hull a dull cherry-red in color. Crewmen aboard the *Texas* could hear the wounded shrieking in terror as the flames neared them. Sailors, many with their clothes aflame, leaped overboard. The *Texas*'s crew cheered wildly, but Captain John Philip quickly brought them to their senses. "Don't cheer, boys!" he called through his megaphone "Those poor devils are dying!"

The cheering continued, only now it was for their comrades from the *Iowa*. As soon as *Vizcaya* went out of action, *Iowa*, the nearest American vessel, tried to rescue the survivors. Life preservers were thrown to men floundering in the water. Marine sharpshooters kept the sharks away from the wounded; they'd come from all directions, attracted by the blood. One lifeboat pulled alongside the wreck. The ship was abandoned, save for three men who stood on the blazing deck, too frightened to move. Suddenly an unidentified sailor stood up in the lifeboat. He was remembering the *Maine* in a special way. When that battleship exploded, Spanish seamen had risked their lives to save her crew. Now he was returning the favor. Without orders, he climbed up a ladder, kicked the three men overboard, and dove after them.

Meantime, the cruiser *Oquendo* and the destroyers *Plutón* and *Furor* were practically blown out of the water. Only the *Cristóbal Colón*, Spain's newest and fastest cruiser, remained.

Cristóbal Colón was in the clear, speeding westward, when the *Oregon* took up the chase. The *Oregon* was fast for a battleship, but she couldn't be expected to overtake a cruiser with a lead of several miles. But *Oregon*'s black gang began to shovel faster, raising the steam pressure in

George Varian's sketch of American
sailors rescuing the crew of the burning
Spanish cruiser Oquendo during the
naval battle of Santiago.

her boilers. Suddenly she showed "a bone in her teeth,"
sailor slang for the two great waves that roll up from the
bow as a ship gains speed. She was doing eighteen knots,
a record for American battleships.

It took an hour, but *Oregon* finally came within range of
the *Cristóbal Colón*. Her crew could hardly control its excitement. An old-timer stationed high in a crow's nest
leaned out and yelled impatiently: "Oh, captain, I say,
can't you give her a thirteen-inch shell, for God's sake!"

Captain Charles Clark did just that. A thirteen-incher
exploded at *Cristóbal Colón*'s stern. Instantly her flag came
down, a sign of surrender, and she headed for the shallows. The battle was over.

It was a victory to match Admiral Dewey's at Manila
Bay. Every enemy vessel had been sunk or captured. Of

the 2,225 men who'd sailed with Cervera, 323 were dead, 151 wounded and 1,670 captured, including the Admiral himself, who'd been picked up from the beach. American losses were one killed, aboard the *Brooklyn,* and two or three slightly wounded. None of the ships was badly damaged.

Victory was the navy's Fourth of July gift to the American people, and they loved it. Once again the bluejackets had come through. Wherever they appeared, they were mobbed, kissed, and carried on men's shoulders.

Santiago was doomed. Cut off from outside aid, there was no hope of rescue. Already ammunition was low and food supplies running out. Refugees were fleeing to the countryside in droves each day. The city's military commander, General José Torel, knew that it was only a matter of time before he'd have to surrender.

The Americans were also suffering. Although General Miles arrived with reinforcements during the second week of July, living conditions were worse than ever. Food was still scarce, and the drinking water came from muddy streams or a pond said to contain Spanish bodies. Doughboys had been unable to change their clothes for three weeks. "I do not at all mind other men's clothes being offensive to me," one explained, "but when I cannot go to sleep on account of my own it grows serious."

A full night's sleep was impossible anyhow. It rained every night, forcing those in the trenches to lie with only their heads and shoulders above the liquid mud. Those behind the firing line wrapped their clothes in rubber ponchos and stood about naked until sunrise. General Miles was shocked when he visited a camp one morning.

He found hundreds of naked men standing at attention and saluting him as he rode past. A camp song captured the soldiers' feelings at this time:

> *Snakes as long as a city street,*
> *Flies and skeeters that can't be beat.*
> *Oh, how we want to leave Cuba,*
> *Lord how we want to go home!*

About the time Miles arrived, a new threat appeared. Army doctors were used to treating boils and rashes; even the deadly typhoid fever and malaria were familiar to them. But now the morning sick call brought patients with high fever and a yellow cast to the skin. Doctors

The American high command in Cuba. Left to right are Generals "Fighting Joe" Wheeler, William R. Shafter, and Nelson A. Miles.

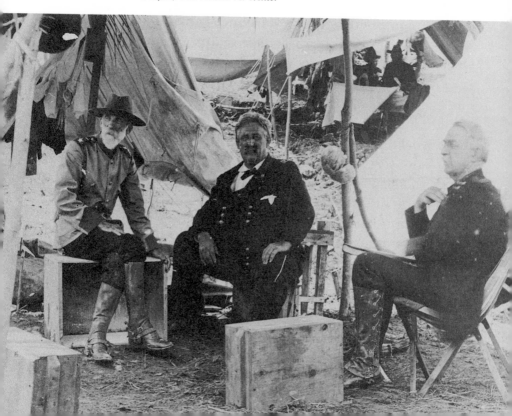

whispered the diagnosis among themselves: yellow fever. Slowly, for the moment at least, "Yellow Jack" was spreading through the ranks.

On July 10, a truce was declared to allow the commanders to discuss surrender terms. General Torel would gladly have surrendered, except that Spanish "honor" forbid it as long as a commander had weapons and the men to use them. If he gave up too easily, he'd lose face; brother officers would shun him as a coward for the rest of his life. Moreover, commanders who surrendered too quickly might face a firing squad.

Torel and Shafter haggled for three days, unable to agree on "honorable" surrender terms. Shafter, who'd found the strength to leave his cot, said it would be easier to have teeth pulled than to face this stubborn Spaniard. Finally, Secretary of War Alger found the solution. In return for Santiago's surrender, he offered to send the Spanish garrison home at United States government expense. As a sign of respect, the Spanish officers could keep their horses and swords; soldiers' weapons would be sent on a separate ship. Torel accepted the terms on July 15 and the Spaniards surrendered two days later.

The surrender, however, did not go smoothly, thanks to the *New York Journal.* Shafter had barred newsmen from the official ceremony. But when he rode into Santiago with his staff, they found posters pasted up along the main streets: *"Remember the Maine! Buy the Journal!"* Willie Hearst's men had entered the city ahead of him. Furious, he went to the city hall to see the raising of Old Glory.

What he saw there made his blood boil. Standing on the roof beside the flagpole was Sylvester Scovel, one of Hearst's star reporters. A general's order meant nothing to

Scovel when it came to getting a juicy story. This time, however, he'd gone too far. When soldiers hustled him into the street, he was so angry at this insult to the "dignity of the press" that he ran up to Shafter and threw a punch at his nose. Shafter then swung at him. Both men missed, although the general had the last word. Scovel was hauled off to jail, where he spent the night in a dark dungeon swarming with rats and roaches. Next morning, he was put on a ship and told never to show his face at headquarters.

The Cuban campaign was over. Although some 190,000 Spanish troops still remained, they were not a serious threat. Most were in the Havana area, bottled up by the guerrillas and an American naval squadron. On July 27, the Spanish government requested a cease-fire and the start of peace talks.

General Miles invaded Puerto Rico a day before the Spanish request arrived in Washington. Actually, it was more of a summer outing than a military operation. When doughboys arrived at Ponce on the southern coast, the *Puertoriqueños* welcomed them as old friends. Once ashore, they fanned out across the island. Some places were so eager to be rid of the Spaniards that they surrendered to the first American they saw. When, for example, Richard Harding Davis reached the town of Coamo ahead of the troops, the mayor surrendered to him and held a fiesta. Stephen Crane "captured" the village of Juana Díaz single-handedly. The Spaniards put up only a halfhearted resistance, and within a few days the island was securely in American hands.

Although the Spaniards were defeated, a deadlier enemy arose in their place. Yellow fever struck with full force during the last week of July. On July 24 doctors reported 396 men down with the disease. The number increased to 500 on July 25 and to 2,924 on July 27. Next day, 4,122 men were sick, of whom 3,193 had "Yellow Jack." In other words, nearly one-quarter of the American army at Santiago was sick and in danger of dying.

Medical science did not know what caused yellow fever or how to cure it. All the doctors could do was to make patients comfortable while nature took its course. Either they died or they recovered on their own. The only hope of preventing the disease from spreading was to move the army out of Cuba to a cooler place.

The War Department saw things differently. It wanted the army to occupy Santiago and the surrounding area until a peace treaty was signed. When Shafter pointed out the dangers of this plan, he was told to keep quiet and obey orders.

On August 3, Shafter's commanders decided there was no time to lose. T. R. wrote a letter that was circulated among his fellow officers. Known as the "round-robin" letter because each officer signed it in turn, it pulled no punches. "This Army must be moved at once or it will perish as an Army," it said bluntly. Shafter was happy to send the letter to Washington without comment. Orders arrived next day to move the army to Montauk Point on Long Island, New York. On August 7, the first troop transports sailed from Santiago. Only yellow fever patients were left behind for fear of bringing the infection to the United States. When—*if*—they recovered, they would also be sent home. Meantime, they'd be cared for in tent hospitals at Siboney.

Blacks played an important role at this time. During the

Despite discrimination at home and in the army, blacks served with great courage and devotion during the Spanish-American War. The troopers in this photo took part in the battle for San Juan Hill.

fighting, black troopers had earned the respect of both friend and foe. At El Caney, the Twenty-Fifth Infantry led frontal assaults on enemy strongpoints. The Ninth Cavalry stormed San Juan Hill alongside white regiments. Had it not been for the Tenth Cavalry, the Rough Riders would probably never have reached the top of Kettle Hill. T.R. said there were no better comrades in a hard fight and called them "an excellent breed of Yankee." The Spaniards were also impressed with their courage, calling them "Smoked Yankees."

Now that the battles were over, blacks faced another challenge. Eight white regiments had refused to work in the yellow fever hospitals. It was dangerous work, and, besides, they were homesick. The all-black Twenty-Fourth Infantry was equally homesick, but its troops volunteered for the assignment. Thanks to them, many soldiers lived to return to their loved ones. The blacks, however, paid a high price for their devotion. Of the 471 men who'd volunteered, only 27 were fit for duty when their services were no longer needed. The others were either sick or had died of yellow fever and other diseases.

The army remained at Montauk Point for six weeks. Its health restored, on September 28 the regulars were given new assignments or returned to their old posts. Volunteer units, among them the Rough Riders, were disbanded. Before heading west, some of T.R.'s men visited New York City. They'd never seen anything like it and, in their excitement, emptied their six-shooters from the Brooklyn Bridge. Stranded in the city without money, three men spent the night in a funeral parlor; the kindly manager offered them three coffins, which proved more restful than the San Juan trenches.

The moment T.R. traded his khaki uniform for a business suit, he began another adventure. He was a national hero, and the Republican Party saw him as a shoe-in for high office. In the fall of 1898, he became the party's candidate for governor of New York State. The governorship, he said, was the highest office he could dream of holding. If he won the election, he didn't care if he never held another. As it turned out, that nomination was a giant step toward the White House.

One of T.R.'s friends was John Hay, the United States ambassador to England. When the Cuban campaign ended, Hay called it "a splendid little war." It probably was that for him, but he'd never dodged Mauser bullets or slept in mud.

The doughboys, however, knew better. Like all wars, it was nasty, brutal, and deadly. Not that it was especially costly; indeed, it caused little loss of life. "Only" 345 Americans were killed in combat. Yet this was only part of the story. The real horror of Cuba was the 5,462 men who'd died of disease. Many—perhaps most—of these deaths were needless. The dead were victims of stupidity and carelessness at the highest levels of government and the military. The lack of medical supplies was simply criminal, and there was no reason to send men into the jungle in woolens or to feed them embalmed beef.

Those who returned from Cuba had a bellyful of war. One volunteer spoke for many after he'd been with his family for a few weeks. If there was another war, he said, he'd cheer the volunteers and tell them to "give 'em one for me." But he'd stay home with the wife and kids.

V
Conquest of the Philippines

"O Dewey at Manila
That fateful first of May,
When you sank the Spanish fleet
In almost bloodless fray.
O glorious Dewey say,
Why didn't you weigh anchor
And softly sail away?"
—Anonymous, c. 1899

Those who cheered Admiral Dewey's victory at Manila Bay might not have been so happy had they been able to see into the future. Without realizing it, Dewey had set the stage for another war, one far more terrible than the struggle in Cuba. Officially known as the Philippine Insurrection, it is the least known of all our wars. History texts seldom discuss it, and if they do, it is covered in a few sentences. Yet it was one of the longest wars ever fought by the United States, lasting from 1899 to 1902. It was also one of the most vicious, with atrocities committed on both sides. Like Vietnam seventy years later, it divided Americans, raising doubts about their commitment to the ideals upon which the republic is based.

The Philippines could have been the planet Mars, for all Americans knew about them when Dewey arrived. Discovered by Ferdinand Magellan in 1521, they are an

133

Okinawa

CHINA

TAIWAN

SOUTH CHINA SEA

PACIFIC OCEAN

T H E

P H I L I P P I N E S

LUZON

Lingayen Gulf

Subic Bay
Bataan Peninsula
Corregidor I.

Manila

MINDORO

SAMAR
Balangiga

PANAY

PALAWAN

LEYTE
Cebu

NEGROS

SULU SEA

NORTH BORNEO

Sulu Archipelago

Sarangani Bay

MINDAN

Map by Virginia Norey

archipelago, or chain of islands, stretching a thousand miles from north to south. The first Spanish settlers came in 1565 and named them for King Philip II—hence the Philippines.

The Philippines consist of 7,073 islands, mostly too small to be shown on maps. The two largest islands are Luzon and Mindanao, roughly equal in size to Illinois and Indiana. The archipelago is inhabited by peoples of various backgrounds, of which the majority are descended from the Malays, a people who came from the Asian mainland about two thousand years ago. Chinese traders arrived soon after, settling among the Malays and intermarrying with them. In addition, scores of primitive tribes lived in the interior. One of these tribes, the Negrito, resemble Africans, though scientists say they are not related. Both the swarthy Malays and the brown-skinned Negritos have jet-black hair.

The Philippines were a treasure house of natural resources. Fertile valleys and plains produced rice, sugar cane, and spices. Hemp, a strong fiber used in making rope, is still a valuable export. Metals such as gold, silver, copper, tin, lead, and iron are found on some islands. There are also deposits of minerals like sulphur, coal, and salt. Fishing has always been a major industry.

The Spaniards exploited the Philippines as they did their older colonies in the New World. Millions of acres of land were stolen from the Filipinos and given to the settlers. Filipinos were worked like oxen and forced to pay high taxes. Native religions were forbidden and the Roman Catholic Church given a religious monopoly. The only religion that resisted the invaders was Islam, which still dominates on the smaller southern islands. Manila, the capital, was built by the Spanish on Luzon and defended by military bases.

By the 1890s, the Philippines had eight million inhabitants. Most Filipinos still lived in barrios, small villages of wooden huts raised on stilts to avoid prowling animals and floods. To enter a hut, you climbed a ladder, then pulled it up if you didn't want company. Travel between barrios was difficult. Flimsy bridges, little more than rope walkways floored with rough planks, swayed over the rivers. There were two types of road: *malos caminos* (bad roads) and *muy malos caminos* (very bad roads). There was only one railroad, a 120-mile line running north from Manila.

Like the Cubans, the Filipinos resented Spanish rule. Patriots formed the *Katipunan,* or Sons of the People, to work for their country's independence. The Katipunan's leader was Emilio Aguinaldo. Born into a prosperous landowning family in 1869, the short, wiry Aguinaldo had to quit school and help run the family business when his father died. But although the business did well, his mind was elsewhere. Aguinaldo believed it was his destiny to lead the Filipinos to freedom. During the 1890s, he joined the Katipunan and helped it to form secret fighting groups. Thanks to his skill as an organizer, he quickly became head of the organization.

The Katipunan believed that only force could make the Spaniards leave their country. In 1896, it began raiding army barracks and assassinating government officials. To end the rebellion, the Spaniards decided to make a deal. After hard bargaining, they promised reforms and offered Aguinaldo and his aides 800,000 pesos if they'd leave the islands. The rebel leaders took the money and sailed for

Hong Kong. But once they'd gone, the Spaniards cracked down harder than ever. No reforms were made, and rebel sympathizers were executed by the hundreds. Aguinaldo planned another uprising—only this time he'd have a powerful ally.

Aguinaldo was in Hong Kong when Dewey's squadron arrived there in April 1898. Both men believed in the adage, "The enemy of my enemy is my friend." And both men needed each other. The Filipino wanted the American's support for his independence struggle against Spain. The American was neither for nor against Filipino independence. He had a job to do—defeat Spain—and wanted Aguinaldo's help in getting it done as easily as possible. Dewey led him to believe that the Americans wanted only to free his country, as they were about to free Cuba. Once that was done, they'd leave, binding their two nations in brotherhood forever. Aguinaldo wished him well when he sailed for Manila Bay.

Dewey's victory, however, did not end Spanish resistance. Although he blockaded Manila, the enemy still held the islands themselves. In order to finish the job, he sent a message to Washington requesting thousands of troops. Since it would take weeks for troops to arrive, Dewey asked Aguinaldo to go ashore and form a Filipino army. There would be no problem about guns, Dewey said; he'd arm them with captured Spanish rifles. The army's mission was to keep the enemy off balance until American troops appeared.

Things went better than Dewey expected. No sooner did Aguinaldo land than Filipinos flocked to his camp at Cavite. What followed was a true war of national liberation. Aguinaldo attacked the Spaniards everywhere. By

mid-June, he'd driven the enemy into Manila, blockading it by land as Dewey had done by sea. Aguinaldo also found time to write a Philippine Declaration of Independence, form a government, and design a national flag. The flag's colors were red, white, and blue, symbolizing his love for the United States.

American troops were then on the high seas. Three contingents, totaling eighteen thousand men, had sailed from San Francisco in June and July. Commanded by Major General Wesley Merritt, an experienced Indian fighter, they were mostly youngsters from ranches and small towns in the West. They'd enlisted for the glorious fight in Cuba and felt cheated by being sent to God-only-knew-where.

Crossing the Pacific was just as nasty as sailing to

Emilio Aguinaldo, first President of the Philippines, led his people in their struggle against American domination.

Cuba. Troopships were overcrowded, dirty and hot; one private said his sleeping quarters were three degrees hotter than hell. Men who'd been at home on bucking broncos became seasick from the constant rocking motion of their ships. Supplies, as usual, were a scandal. Those with complete uniforms wore the standard blue sweatsuits. Others made do with whatever they could find. An Oregon regiment, for example, wore their civilian shoes, since army boots were unavailable; other men had no underwear. Instead of embalmed beef, Philippines-bound soldiers ate "goldfish," fatty salmon in a thick, greasy sauce. The ships swarmed with "graybacks," or lice, tiny crablike insects that made them miserable.

On June 20, the ships anchored off the Spanish island of Guam. After a few shots, a boat carrying the Spanish commander put out from shore and approached the flagship, the cruiser *Charleston*. The Spaniard apologized for his rudeness; since he had no big guns, he said, he couldn't return the visitors' "salute." Only then did he learn that his country was at war. By sunset, he and his seventy men were securely locked in *Charleston*'s brig. The United States had seized its first Pacific island. During World War II, Guam would be the scene of American battles against the Japanese.

The first contingent reached Manila early in July, just as Aguinaldo was preparing an all-out assault. When they landed, Dewey persuaded the rebel leader to let the U.S. take over part of the Filipino front line. After all, they were friends, and friends must help one another against the common enemy.

Although Aguinaldo agreed, he was uncomfortable. The American attitude raised questions in his mind. So

A group of soldiers loyal to Emilio Aguinaldo fall in for inspection on the island of Luzon.

far, they hadn't recognized his Philippine Republic. Why were there so many troops, now that he was about to take the city on his own? What were the Americans' true intentions? Could they be trusted?

Aguinaldo's suspicions were justified. Everything the Americans did—or *didn't* do—had a reason. Even before the troops sailed, President McKinley had decided to take over the Philippines. He did so, not out of selfishness, but for the good of both peoples, he said. McKinley believed that the Filipinos were backward, incapable of self-government. They might be ready for it in a hundred years, but now they needed American protection and guidance. If we got rid of the Spaniards and then sailed away, the islands would only fall to another power, one not as generous as the United States. England and Germany had already shown interest in them; Japan too wanted to control them. The islands were also vital to American trade in Asia and the Pacific. Philippine bases would enable the navy to keep the sea lanes open for our merchant shipping.

Dewey and Merritt were ordered to take Manila before a peace treaty was signed. General Firmín Jaudenes, the Spanish governor, knew the city was lost, but that Spanish "honor" would not allow surrender without a battle. He also knew that he had to surrender to the Americans— and do it fast. The Filipinos had scores to settle with their oppressors. If the rebels captured the city, there was a good chance that they'd massacre the garrison.

The American commanders gave Jaudenes an offer he couldn't refuse. Going behind Aguinaldo's back, they agreed to stage a fake battle. It would be a grand show, but a show nevertheless.

On August 13, Dewey's ships fired on one of the strongest Spanish forts. It was a slow fire, answered slowly by the enemy's shore batteries. No ships were damaged, but the fort took several direct hits. After an hour, the guns fell silent to allow the American troops to advance. Not a shot was fired as they came forward. Reaching the fort, they found it empty. Advancing further, they discovered thousands of Spanish soldiers waiting for them under white flags. General Jaudenes had surrendered with honor after a "battle." The Americans quickly occupied Manila. When Filipino troops tried to enter the city, they found the way barred by doughboys. Aguinaldo was told that they would not be allowed in, and that the city would remain in American hands until a peace treaty decided the fate of the Philippines. The Filipino leader felt betrayed, as he in fact had been. But this was only the beginning.

The peace treaty ending the Spanish-American War was signed by American and Spanish diplomats on December 10, 1898. By its terms, Puerto Rico and Guam were ceded to the United States. Cuba became independent, but American troops would remain until a stable government was established. They were withdrawn in 1903, although Guantanamo Bay is still an American naval base. In return for $20 million, the Philippine Islands became the property of the United States.

Spanish soldiers, now prisoners of war, after the surrender of Manila.

Filipinos were outraged when they learned of the treaty. Aguinaldo knew enough American history to realize that it was a turning point. Once Americans had been ruled against their will by a foreign power. They had rebelled and, since then, had stood for the right of peoples to be free and independent. Now they'd betrayed their own ideals. They'd *bought* the Philippines and the Filipinos like so many sacks of rice and pounds of sugar. On January 6, 1899, Aguinaldo's government broke off friendly relations with United States forces in the islands.

War was coming. Both sides knew it and prepared for it. Both deepened trenches and strengthened barricades. American soldiers shouted insults to Filipino soldiers across the lines. Filipinos tried to draw the fire of American sentries. They'd often dart across the American line, dare the sentries to fire, and run back to their positions. Aguinaldo planned to start the war with an attack on Manila. Detailed orders were issued to his troops and to agents inside the city. The attack must be a complete surprise, he wrote. In order to approach the enemy, men were to dress as women, concealing bolos under their clothes. The bolo is a single-edged machete, razor-sharp and deadly at close quarters. At the moment of attack, "they shall pursue slashing right and left with bolos until the Americans surrender." Those who resisted should be cut down without mercy.

The Americans beat Aguinaldo to the punch. On the evening of February 4, 1899, Private Willie Grayson, First Nebraska Volunteers, was patrolling near a bridge when four Filipino soldiers came out of the darkness.

"Halt!" Grayson shouted.

"Halto!" shouted their lieutenant arrogantly.

"Well," Grayson recalled, "I thought the best thing to do was to shoot him. He dropped." And the war began.

That war is known by two names. Americans call it the Phillipine Insurrection, a rebellion against their lawful authority. Filipinos call it the War for Independence, an honorable struggle for liberty. Today historians in both countries agree that it was an unnecessary war. They also agree in putting most of the blame for it on President McKinley and his advisers. Aguinaldo really did love the United States. Before the war began, he'd promised to give his ally naval bases as well as trading privileges in the islands. But McKinley wouldn't settle for anything less than the islands themselves. He got them—but at what a cost!

Aguinaldo turned against his former ally with a murderous fury. "War without quarter to the false Americans who have deceived us! Either independence or death!" he told his troops. His army numbered eighty thousand men, of whom fewer than half had rifles; and these were poor marksmen. Its artillery was limited to some old Spanish guns and "bamboo cannon," iron pipes that shot nails and broken glass. Every soldier carried a bolo and knew how to use it. One unit consisted of Negritos with bows and arrows. Another was made up of children armed only with stones to throw at the enemy.

Filipinos were no match for Americans in open battle. The American army lacked many things, but it had plenty of weapons, especially artillery. Doughboys were also good shots, having mastered the rifle as boys. They even learned how to "improve" their weapons or make entirely new ones. A soldier, for example, could easily turn a regular bullet into a dum-dum by carving an X into its point so that it would explode inside a victim's body. An artillery battery rigged a fire engine to spray burning kerosene, an early version of the flamethrower.

During the first days' fighting, American artillery shattered the Filipino lines. When their trenches were overrun, some three thousand dead were counted, compared to sixty doughboys. From then on, it was one victory after another. American forces broke out of Manila and attacked in all directions. Wherever they struck, the enemy collapsed. Success came so easily that doughboys began to take it for granted. For them, the war became a glorified hunting party. Picking off Filipinos, a private wrote his parents, was "more fun than a turkey shoot." Another wrote that dead Filipinos lay on the ground "thicker than buffalo chips."

Defeat unleashed a cruel streak in the Filipinos. Cap-

Filipino insurgents lying where they fell in a skirmish with American troops on February 5, 1899.

tured Americans were shown no mercy. The "lucky" ones were kept tied up for days on end, beaten, and starved. To humiliate a man, a Filipino might hold his head between his hands and spit full in his face. Sometimes Filipinos toyed with their captives: they'd point pistols at their heads and pull the triggers on empty chambers. The victims, not knowing if the weapons were loaded, were scared out of their wits. Unlucky prisoners had their ears and noses cut off and salt forced into the bleeding wounds. Doughboys were buried up to their necks and their faces smeared with sweet syrups to attract ants; by the time the ants had finished, only an empty skull remained. On one occasion, as American troops neared an enemy camp, prisoners were forced to kneel and were hacked to pieces with bolos.

The doughboys answered in kind. Yet in doing so, they broke laws that are as old as the United States. Even under battle conditions, soldiers must protect enemy civilians and their property, insofar as it does not endanger their own lives. Enemy wounded must be cared for as if they were Americans; prisoners must be well-treated. Anyone who acts otherwise is a criminal and liable to prison or the hangman's rope.

Soldiers in the Philippines often broke the law and were allowed to do so by their officers. Cruelty begets cruelty. Troops would go wild after finding mutilated buddies. Then nothing stood in the way of their revenge. Villages were burnt. Enemy soldiers were not allowed to surrender, or were shot after surrendering. The wounded were killed. "We killed them like rabbits. . . . Everyone was crazy," said a trooper from Seattle, Washington. By 1900, fifteen Filipinos were being killed for every wounded one who reached a prison camp. During the American Civil War, five soldiers were wounded for every one killed, which is about normal in modern warfare. Clearly, doughboys were not trying to save the injured Filipinos.

Some officers ordered criminal actions to teach the enemy a lesson. Private A. A. Barnes of the Third Artillery wrote about one officer to his brother in Indiana. "Last night one of our boys was found shot and his stomach cut open. Immediately orders were received from [our general] to burn the town and kill every native in sight; which was done. . . . Tell all my inquiring friends that I am doing everything for Old Glory and for the America I love so well." The name of the town was Titatia. A thousand men, women, and children were slaughtered there within a few hours.

Many such letters were written during the Philippine Insurrection. They were shown to friends and neighbors back home and printed in local newspapers. Some may be read today in the Library of Congress. It was hard to be ignorant about the crimes being committed in America's name.

The need for information also led to cruelty. Armies without information are merely blundering mobs bound to suffer casualties, even lose the war. Enemy prisoners are a major source of information. Soldiers, though they are taught not to reveal what they know, must be persuaded to talk.

The water cure was the doughboys' favorite "persuader." A prisoner was thrown on his back, held down, and his mouth forced open with a stick. A bucket of water was then poured down his throat. He might kick and moan, but the water kept coming until his belly swelled to the bursting point. When it could hold no more water, a soldier knelt beside him and asked questions. If he refused to answer, someone stood on his stomach. One soldier told how "a good heavy man" jumped on a prisoner's stomach, "sending a gush of water from his mouth into the air as high as six feet." The torture continued until he talked or died. Most talked. This was a cruel method, yet it was not used for sport and it saved American lives. Information forced from prisoners did reveal enemy plans and lead to the capture of hidden weapons. Doughboys felt that the ends, however illegal, justified the means. Their leaders must have agreed, since no one was ever punished for giving the water cure.

Racism was perhaps the most important reason for cruelty. Too many Americans brought the racism they'd learned at home to the Philippines. They referred to the Filipinos as "goo-goos" and "niggers." Filipinos were "subhumans" to them, hardly members of the human race. Indeed, it seemed to them the only good Filipino was a dead Filipino. Doughboys, marching with their Krag-Jörgensen rifles, expressed this idea in a ferocious song:

> Damn, damn, damn the Filipino,
> Cut-throat khakiac ladrone!*
> Underneath the starry flag,
> Civilize him with a Krag,
> And returns us to our beloved home.

General Shafter demanded the extermination of Aguinaldo's followers, even if that meant killing half the Fili-

*A khakiac ladrone was a native bandit.

pino people: "Then I would treat the rest of them with perfect justice."

The racism of white American soldiers was resented by their black comrades. All black regiments in the Philippines had served in Cuba. They'd served honorably, and five of their members won the Medal of Honor for courage above and beyond the call of duty. That meant nothing to the majority of whites. Blacks, as well as Filipinos, were targets of racial insults. Since both were dark-skinned, both were equally "niggers."

Aguinaldo tried to exploit the blacks soldiers' resentments. He personally designed posters and wrote pamphlets urging them to desert from the army. Blacks, he said, mustn't serve a nation that despised them. They should join their true friends, the Filipinos, in a common struggle for justice. Even Filipino children helped to carry this message. William Simms, a black sergeant, was asked by a boy: "Why does the American Negro come from America to fight us when we are such a friend to him and have not done anything to him? He is all the same as me and me all the same as you. Why don't you fight those people in America who burn Negroes, that make a beast of you?"

Like the vast majority of black soldiers, Simms remained loyal. Racism hurt, but it wasn't the whole story. Whatever America's faults, it was still his country.

Nine men, however, did go over to the enemy. The most feared deserter was Private David Fagen of the Twenty-Fourth Infantry. Fagen ran off with all the pistols he could carry and became a captain in the Filipino army. For two years he trained Filipinos in the use of rifles and sent appeals to other blacks to follow his example. One day he was assigned to guard several white American prisoners. As he was marching them into the jungle, shots were heard; he'd killed them, he said, when they tried to "escape." Bigots claimed that Fagen proved blacks were disloyal and unworthy of having the same rights as white people. This charge was ridiculous, given the record of the black fighting man.

Back home, many people who'd welcomed a war over Cuba condemned the Philippine Insurrection. Early in 1899, a number of them formed the Anti-Imperialist League. League members believed that the war violated American ideals. The Declaration of Independence, they claimed, was not just for Americans. God meant for all people, of whatever race or color, to enjoy life, liberty, and the pursuit of happiness. The Philippine war was immoral and criminal. It must be stopped immediately.

Some prominent people became League members. Among them were ex-presidents Benjamin Harrison and Grover Cleveland; Samuel Gompers, president of the American Federation of Labor; and the presidents of Harvard and Stanford Universities. Andrew Carnegie, the richest man in America, offered to write a personal check for $20 million to buy Philippine independence.

Mark Twain, the humorist and creator of Tom Sawyer and Huck Finn, was an outspoken Anti-Imperialist. Yet there was nothing funny about his opinions on the war. America, he wrote, should hide her head in shame. "[W]e have crushed and deceived a confiding people; we have turned against the weak and the friendless who trusted us; we have stamped out a just and intelligent and well-ordered republic; we have stabbed an ally in the back; . . . we have robbed a trusting friend of his land and his liberty; we have invited our clean young men . . . to do bandits' work . . . ; we have blackened [America's] face before the world." Mark Twain was so bitter that he wanted to do away with the Stars and Stripes. America deserved a new flag, he said, one in which the white stripes were painted black and the stars replaced by the pirate's skull and crossbones.

Some Anti-Imperialists adopted methods that would become widespread during the Vietnam War. They praised the enemy and wished him well, while damning their own elected leaders. Rallies were held in which Aguinaldo was cheered and McKinley hissed. The president, they said, was a cold-blooded murderer, a beast ignorant of right and wrong. Protesters blocked army recruiting stations to discourage volunteers. Garbage was collected in an American flag during an anti-war demonstration in Boston.

And as in the Vietnam War, protesters were called traitors by those who disagreed with them. Army officers wrote from the Philippines, accusing them of giving aid and comfort to the enemy. In this case, the charges were correct. By their own words, protesters hoped for a Filipino victory and an American defeat. Captured documents reveal that their activities raised Aguinaldo's hopes and encouraged him to continue fighting against all odds. He later admitted that, owing to the protests, "we hoped that the American people would soon demand an end to the war."

In the first months of the twentieth century, the war did seem to be ending. From January to May 1900, American forces occupied every inhabited island in the archipelago. On Luzon, the Filipino army was defeated and its remnants driven into the hills. American commanders were optimistic, predicting complete victory by summer. They were wrong. Far from being over, the hardest fighting still lay ahead.

Aguinaldo gave up trying to defeat the Americans in open battle. They were too strong, too stubborn, to be forced out of the Philippines against their will. He hoped to help them to change their minds by wearing them out, making their occupation as costly as possible. Then, they'd be only too glad to leave. Ironically, his plan would put the U.S. in the same position as "Butcher" Weyler in Cuba. In order to win, Americans would have to adopt his methods—the very methods that had triggered the Spanish-American War.

The Filipino leader went into hiding at a jungle camp somewhere in Luzon. No longer would the Filipinos fight in large units, but in small bands, guerrilla-style. The islands were divided into guerrilla zones, each commanded by a general, whom Aguinaldo directed through a system of codes and messengers. But he never showed himself, never led in person, since his capture would have meant the end of Filipino resistance. His hideout was so secret that not even his top generals knew its location.

The guerrillas struck only when and where they chose. They'd raid American supply columns when least expected, cut telegraph lines, and ambush small detachments. One ambush ended in the capture of a fifty-one-man company, the largest surrender of U.S. troops since the Civil War. Another took the life of Major General Henry W. Lawton. The highest-ranking American officer to be killed during the war, Lawton had led the assault on El Caney.

Masters at setting booby traps, guerrillas made every trail an avenue of death. Their favorite trap was a deep pit covered with straw and filled with *pungis,* sharpened stakes to impale anyone who fell on them. Some used poisoned spears instead of stakes. The poison was easily made; you simply smeared the spearhead in manure and let the bacteria do the rest. The wound became infected, putting the victim out of action for weeks; many died of blood poisoning.

If an American commander tried to retaliate, he was beaten before he started. It was impossible to keep secrets, since the occupied areas swarmed with spies. As soon as they saw troops preparing to leave, the villagers sent word to the local guerrilla band. If the troops came too close for comfort, the band vanished without firing a shot. Its members hid their weapons, went to work in the nearest field, and shouted, *"Viva America"*—"Long live America"—at the passing doughboys. Then, when the coast was clear, they grabbed their weapons and swung into action. American soldiers hated these tactics. Filipinos didn't fight fair, like real men, they said. "Damn 'em," cried one general, "they won't stand up to be shot!"

The Americans controlled only the ground they stood upon; everything else belonged to the guerrillas. Each barrio actually had two governments. The first was appointed by, and responsible to, the Americans. It operated in public and had little power. The second was appointed by Aguinaldo's men. It operated secretly and had the power of life and death.

The secret government was run by a committee loyal to Aguinaldo. It existed to serve the guerrillas in any way it could. Committee tax collectors collected money and supplies for them. Committee recruiters sent them fighting men, guides, and lookouts. Committee members cared for their wounded and hid their messengers. Committee police kept the barrio loyal to the cause.

The police ruled by terror. They left no doubt that anyone who cooperated with the Americans risked their own and their family's lives. At first, policemen made threats; for example, a suspect's dog might be killed and its blood smeared on the door of his house. If threats didn't work, the murder squad took over. Punishment was made as horrible as possible as an example to others. In 1900, for example, 350 officials appointed by the Americans were assassinated, often in front of their wives and children. Ordinary people were clubbed to death, decapitated, or buried alive. In one village a "traitor" was tied to a post and an American flag wrapped around his head. The flag was then doused with kerosene and set afire. The men watched without showing emotion, but the women and children pressed their fingers to their ears to shut out his screams.

Terrorism paid off. Americans found that most Filipinos would have nothing to do with them. They refused to accept government jobs; and those who did spied for the guerrillas. Villagers would sooner take the water cure than betray the guerrillas. American morale began to sag as their losses mounted. Always tense, trusting no one, fearing everyone, doughboys never knew when death would strike at them from the shadows. They even began to lose faith in themselves. An army song of 1900 ends with this question:

I'd like to know who's the boss of this show,
Is it me or Emilio Aguinaldo?

The answer came the following year.

Early in 1901, the Americans set out to break the guerrillas once and for all. Their plan was a combination of gentle and harsh methods. Gentle methods were to win the people's loyalty by improving their lives. Harsh methods would severely punish them for disloyalty. A similar plan, updated and enlarged, was tried by American forces during the Vietnam War. It failed in Vietnam but was a brilliant success in the Philippines.

The plan was to be carried out by a civilian governor and a military governor, both appointed by President McKinley. Judge William Howard Taft of Ohio was the civilian governor. "Big Bill" Taft, later the twenty-sixth president of the United States, weighed 350 pounds. A respected lawyer, he had a keen mind and an ability to view a problem from every angle. Major General Arthur MacArthur was the military governor. A Medal of Honor winner at eighteen, he'd earned the rank of colonel during some of the worst fighting of the Civil War. "Mac" was all soldier: smart, tough, daring. So was his son, Douglas, who commanded American forces in the Pacific during World War II.

Taft realized that Filipinos would abandon the guerrillas only if they trusted the Americans and saw them as

General Arthur
McArthur broke
the back of Filipino
resistance during the
Philippine Insurrection.
His son, Douglas, led
American forces to victory
in the Pacific during the
Second World War.

friends. To build that trust, he created America's first "Peace Corps." Village schools were built and teachers brought from the mainland. Not only did they teach their subjects, they trained natives to carry on their work in remote areas.

Epidemic diseases, an age-old scourge in the islands, were brought under control. Public health officers led village cleanup campaigns, arranged for garbage disposal, and purified water supplies. Doctors, many of them off-duty army surgeons, set up clinics and vaccinated people against smallpox, which had once wiped out entire villages. Quinine, a drug used to treat malaria, was given free to anyone in need.

Engineers built bridges and roads, improved harbors and drained swamps, useful projects that gave jobs to the poor and earned their gratitude. Taft also set up a system of local self-government based on democratic principles. All villages were to elect their officials and have their own police forces.

These measures began to win Filipino "hearts and

minds." In one village after another, people took the oath of loyalty to the United States. In some places, they even turned in Aguinaldo's commanders. The guerrillas, seeing their power challenged, struck back. But this time the Americans were ready.

General MacArthur was a pioneer in "counterinsurgency," the art of fighting guerrillas. He began by announcing that their cause was lost; the Americans would never leave the Philippines. Therefore, those who continued to fight were not soldiers serving any government. They were common criminals and would be treated as such when captured. This was no idle threat, as Filipinos quickly discovered. "Mac" made sure that those who helped the guerrillas with money and supplies lost their property and received long jail terms. Anyone who killed an American prisoner or assassinated an official was executed as a murderer. Former officials in Aguinaldo's government were deported to Guam.

Reinforcements poured in from the United States, raising the number of troops under MacArthur's command to over seventy thousand. Several thousand of these were sent to keep order in the villages. Most, however, were to hunt the guerrilla bands on their own ground. They were aided by the Division of Military Information. Organized by MacArthur, the DMI blanketed the country with paid spies and informers. Captured Filipino documents were sent to DMI headquarters in Manila for study; a special unit decoded them if necessary. The water cure continued, but became less important than the orderly gathering of information by trained agents.

MacArthur's troops occupied every key point in the islands. Using these as bases, they sent "flying columns" to probe the countryside beyond. Always on the move, the columns went everywhere, allowing the guerrillas no rest. Guerrilla camps were raided, weapons seized, and food destroyed. Ambushes were set in the jungle, giving the guerrillas a taste of their own medicine.

Flying columns were often guided by Macabebe Scouts. Using friendly natives to catch unfriendly natives was a trick learned during the Indian wars. Now it was applied on a far larger scale. The Macabebe were a tribe that hated the Malays and had sided with the Spaniards during the revolution. When Spain lost the islands, they joined the Americans. Known for both courage and cruelty, they struck terror in ordinary Filipinos. The guerrillas usually tortured Macabebe prisoners to death.

Tracking guerrillas was hard, dangerous work. The doughboys walked through tall grass single file, each blade sharp as a sword. It tore their clothes and cut their skin, covering them with scores of small, painful wounds. The jungle teemed with lizards, rats, mice, centipedes, and tarantulas, hairy spiders large as a man's hand. Giant mosquitoes bit through shirts and pants. Most dangerous were the leeches, slimy, wormlike creatures that crawled under one's clothing to suck blood. Troopers scratched the itchy bites with dirty hands or smeared them with mud or tobacco juice, causing serious infections.

Campaigning in the mountains was just as difficult. Corporal Arthur E. Peterson, a black volunteer, wrote his mother about going on patrol and the people he met along the way:

> My company is stationed in this place some three hundred odd miles from Manila; in fact, the whole regiment is somewhere in

the vicinity. We are right in the heart of the mountains, and we have to patrol over them every day, climbing mountains. Now, mountain climbing is not what it's cracked up to be, even under favorable conditions, but when it comes to climbing out here, where someone is shooting at you from behind a tree, or a stone, it is a mess. And, of course, the sun is broiling hot and to make things worse I am on guard every other night; that is, I only get about three nights' sleep a week. And even those three cannot be termed sleep, because someone will fire a shot during the night and then there will be no more sleep for me that night.

American actions severely hurt the guerrillas, but they could never destroy them as long as Aguinaldo remained at large. All efforts to find his hideout had failed until Frederick Funston entered the picture. Funston, a short man with a red face and a beard to match, was the son of an influential Kansas politician. A born adventurer, he quit college to join exploring expeditions to California's Death Valley and Alaska. When the Cuban troubles began, he served as the rebels' chief artillery officer. Twice wounded, he returned home just as the Spanish-American War began. The state governor promptly named him colonel of the Twentieth Kansas Volunteers. Shortly after arriving in the Philippines, he won the Medal of Honor and was promoted to the rank of brigadier general.

In February 1901 Funston's men captured a messenger with letters from Aguinaldo to his commanders in central Luzon. After some strong "persuasion," the man, Cecilio Segismundo, revealed his chief's whereabouts. Aguinaldo was in the village of Palanan in northern Luzon, a wilderness of rugged mountains and dense jungle. It was impossible to surprise him there, since every village for hundreds of miles was on the alert for strangers. The moment an American column entered the area, he'd escape.

Funston worked out a daring scheme. The captured letters showed that Aguinaldo wanted reinforcements, and Funston's plan would make sure he'd get them. Aguinaldo would be supplied with eighty Macabebe Scouts disguised as loyal guerrillas. They'd be accompanied by five "captured" American officers, among them the general himself. Segismundo would accompany them as a guide. He'd be looked after by Lazaro Segovia, a former Spanish secret service agent now working for the Americans. If Segismundo made one false move, it would be his last; Segovia had orders to kill him on the spot. Rather than march the whole way, the task force would be put ashore from a navy ship a hundred miles from Palanan. Marching overland, it would enter the village, take Aguinaldo by surprise, and bring him back to the coast, where they'd meet the ship.

"Funston," said General MacArthur, "I fear I shall never see you again." And after hearing those cheerful words, Funston boarded the *Vicksburg.*

The task force landed on the night of March 14, 1901. For the next nine days, it slogged over rocky beaches, waded swift streams, and scaled steep cliffs. Food nearly ran out, forcing the men to gather snails and small fish, which were stewed with dried corn. Yet there could be no turning back. Funston threatened to shoot anyone who refused to go on. No one refused.

The task force entered Palanan during a birthday celebration for Aguinaldo. The force was saluted by Aguinaldo's guards and personally congratulated by the leader for capturing the American officers. Meantime, Segovia and two others had joined *el presidente* in his house, a two-story building on stilts. "Now is the time, Macabebes! Give it to them!," Segovia shouted from the window. The Macabebes opened fire, sending the guards fleeing into the jungle. Segovia's companions tackled Aguinaldo and sat on him while the Spaniard shot two of his aides with a pistol.

Funston and the other "prisoners" barged into the room moments later. Introducing himself to the Filipino, he promised he'd be safe as long as he followed orders. Aguinaldo was so dazed that he could only ask, "Is this not some joke?"

Aguinaldo was brought to MacArthur's headquarters in Manila. At last he realized that his cause was lost. On April 19 he gave his oath of loyalty to the United States. "There has been enough blood, enough tears, enough desolation," he told the Filipino people. "By acknowledg-

After eluding American patrols for months, Emilio Aguinaldo was captured by Colonel Frederick Funston, and returned to Manila.

ing and accepting the sovereignty of the United States throughout the Philippine Archipelago . . . I believe I am serving thee, my beloved country."* He said that all true Filipinos must lay down their arms and try to get along with their new rulers.

Aguinaldo's appeal took the heart out of the Filipino resistance. Five days after he issued it, fifteen hundred guerrillas surrendered near Manila alone. During the next three months, another sixteen thousand turned themselves in, together with their weapons. Even David Fagen, the black deserter, was put out of action. Filipino bounty hunters brought in his head to collect the six hundred dollar reward that had been offered for his capture dead or alive.

Once again the American military declared an end to the war. And once again they were proven wrong.

Except for holdouts on Samar, the Philippines' third largest island, the guerrilla forces had indeed been broken. But those holdouts fought more fiercely than ever. The American public learned just how fiercely in the fall of 1901.

Company C, Ninth Infantry Regiment, was stationed in the village of Balangiga on the south coast of Samar. On the evening of September 27, a naval vessel arrived with supplies and mail. The troopers hadn't seen a letter or a newspaper from home since their arrival a month before. And what they read that night took them completely by surprise. On September 6, President McKinley

---

*Aguinaldo retired into private life, and always wore a black bow tie in mourning for the lost Philippine Republic. He died in his ninety-fifth year, on February 6, 1964, nearly sixty-five years to the day after the start of the Philippine Insurrection.

had been shot by Leon Czolgosz, an unemployed laborer whose only explanation was "I done my duty." McKinley's successor was none other than Rough Rider Theodore Roosevelt.

Upon leaving the army, T.R. easily won election as governor of New York. In two years in Albany, his ideas about honest government so annoyed the Republican Party bosses that they decided to get rid of him at the first opportunity. Using McKinley's 1900 reelection bid as an excuse, they pushed T.R.'s nomination for the vice-presidency. Roosevelt considered the office a dead end, since vice-presidents do very little and have no real power. He accepted the nomination, however, and because of McKinley's assassination he became the twenty-fifth president of the United States.

Early the next morning, Company C gathered in a mess tent about a hundred feet from their barracks. It was Sunday, a day of rest, and they were taking things easy. Fighting was the last thing on their minds, and their rifles were stacked near their bunks. As some ate breakfast, others discussed the news or sat quietly reading their mail. Native workmen were also up and about, under the watchful eyes of three armed sentries. People strolled in the village square or sat around in small groups, talking among themselves. Then hell broke loose.

The village police chief approached one of the sentries, grabbed his rifle, and smashed him over the head with the butt. Instantly church bells clanged and conch-shell whistles blared. Filipinos took bolos from beneath their clothing and ran toward the mess tent, shrieking like madmen. It was a carefully planned attack, and everything went like clockwork.

Some soldiers never knew what hit them. A sergeant was just bending over to wash his mess tin in a metal barrel filled with boiling water. *Whack!* Someone struck him from behind, cracked his skull, and pitched him head first into the bubbling water. Another man was struck in the face; the bolo sliced off the front of his face from the bridge of the nose to the throat. A boloman swung at a third American, severing his head and sending it into his plate with a plop; his body leaned forward, gushing a fountain of blood, with a spoon still clutched in its hand.

The men of Company C were veterans and they knew how to fight. "Get your rifles, boys!" Sergeant Markley roared. Grabbing anything they could find—kitchen knives, picks, shovels, rocks, baseball bats—they lashed out at their attackers. The company cook threw canned goods, then took a meat cleaver and broke every Filipino head within reach. Slowly they inched toward the barracks. The grassy path became slippery with blood, but they kept going. A survivor later recalled seeing a comrade crawl on his hands and knees, his brains oozing from a long gash in his skull.

Those who reached their Krags opened fire at point-blank range. It wasn't necessary to aim, since the Filipinos kept charging head-on. They fired so fast that the gun barrels became hot and burned their hands; yet they kept shooting, for their lives depended on it. After about an hour they fought their way to the shore and piled into a *baroto,* a large native canoe. The Filipinos gave chase in other *barotos,* but were driven off by a hail of bullets. Sharks circled the craft, waiting for the wounded to slip overboard.

At 3:00 A.M. the next morning, the boat reached an

American outpost on the neighboring island of Leyte. Of the seventy-four officers and men of Company C, only twenty-six remained. Only four were not wounded. No officers survived.

News of Balangiga shocked the American public. People rated it as a disaster to rival the Alamo and Custer's defeat at the Little Big Horn. Headlines condemned the "savagery" of the Samarians and demanded revenge.

Brigadier General Jacob W. Smith provided it. Known as "Hell Roaring Jake" because of his loud voice and fiery temper, Smith had spent thirty-five years fighting Indians. Sent to crush resistance on Samar, he gave one of the most barbaric (and criminal) orders ever issued by an American officer.

Smith visited Balangiga after its recapture from the guerrillas. It had been cleaned up for his visit, but signs of the massacre were to be seen everywhere. Horrified, he told his officers to be merciless toward the natives. All were guilty; none were entitled to protection under the laws of war. "Kill and burn!" he said. "Kill and burn! The more you kill and burn, the better you will please me. I want no prisoners, do you understand?" Everyone capable of carrying a weapon was to be killed, including children over the age of ten. "Samar must be made a howling wilderness."

Smith's officers did *not* kill everyone over ten; that would have been murder. They did, however, devastate Samar. Concentration camps were set up on the coast and all natives living in the interior ordered to report to them. Those who didn't appear within a given time were regarded as enemies and shot on sight. "Search and destroy" operations burned anything that might be useful to the guerrillas. Anyone found with the possessions of Company C members received rough justice. A patrol once stopped at a hut occupied by two women and an old man. The hut contained Army clothes and three blood-stained bolos; all three were shot on the spot.

There was an outcry when Smith's orders became known in the United States. The Army decided to court-martial Smith on charges of violating military discipline, not for ordering his men to commit murder. He was found guilty and sentenced to be "admonished," given a formal letter of disapproval by his superiors. And his highest superior was President Theodore Roosevelt.

T.R. disliked Filipinos, calling them "bloody savages" and "thankless ingrates." The guerrillas had committed awful crimes, he said, and deserved whatever happened to them as a result. If the doughboys sometimes commit-ted similar acts, that was understandable and forgivable, given the enemy's provocation. He strongly approved of Smith's methods; the general's only real crime was his "loose and violent talk." According to Roosevelt, Hell Roaring Jack was right, only he should have kept his mouth shut. Rather than punish such an able officer, the President had him retired from the service at full pension.

"Butcher" Weyler had the last laugh. The United States had gone to war to end Spain's reign of terror in Cuba. Now those very same methods ended the Filipino resist-ance. Thanks to Smith and men like him, the guerrillas of Samar were either dead or behind bars. Quiet settled over the devastated island and its people returned to what was left of their homes. On July 4, 1902, President Roosevelt officially declared the war ended.

The Philippine Insurrection claimed the lives of 4,234

Americans, wounded 2,818 others and cost $600 million, thirty times the original purchase price. At least sixteen thousand Filipino soldiers had been killed in battle; another two hundred thousand civilians died of disease, starvation, and other war-related causes.

Bitterness over the war lingered for decades. During the Japanese occupation of World War II, hundreds of Filipinos collaborated with the invader as a way of avenging the earlier defeat. Although the Philippines were granted independence in 1946, doughboys never forgot Filipino cruelty. During the Vietnam War, surviving doughboys were questioned about their attitudes. Private Jesse Peck, a man in his late eighties, spoke for many of his comrades. He, like they, was still haunted by seventy-year-old nightmares: "I can never forgive them for their treatment of some of my buddies."

The Spanish War and the Philippine Insurrection were small wars with large results. Like America's busy factories and teeming cities, they were part of a national coming-of-age. Isolated, inward-looking America vanished within the space of four years. In place of the former colony stood a world power with colonies of her own and new responsibilities. Yet no one could be sure how she'd use that power or live up to those responsibilities. The answers would come only with time, as the twentieth century unfolded.

Notes

Chapter One

3 "Oh, Jesus . . ." A. C. M. Azoy, *Charge! The Story of the Battle of San Juan Hill,* p. 16.

4 "On the white paint . . ." G. J. A. O'Toole, *The Spanish War,* p. 125f.

13 "Generals June . . ." Philip S. Foner, *The Spanish-Cuban-American War,* pp. 17f; "Blessed be the torch . . ." O'Toole, p. 54

13 *He has a face* . . . Foner, p.74

17 *I travelled by rail* . . . H. Wayne Morgan, *America's Road to Empire,* p. 25.

20 *The force of the newspaper* . . . *Journal,* September 25, 1898.

26 "Spaniards! . . ." Azoy, p. 1of; O'Toole, p. 251.

31 "The President . . ." Jack Cameron Dierks, *A Leap to Arms,*
p. 24.

Chapter Two

42 "He wants to be killing . . ." Gerald F. Linderman, *The Mirror of War,* p. 91f.
43 "All the great masterful races . . ." Edmund Morris, *The Rise of Theodore Roosevelt,* p. 569; "Call the roll . . ." Fletcher Pratt, *The Navy,* p. 364.
49 "Commodore . . ." O'Toole, p. 181f.
51 "Well, Well . . ." Lauren Hall Healy and Luis Kutner, *The Admiral,* p. 177.
54 *The battle hatches . . .* Frank Friedel, *The Splendid Little War,* p. 23.
60 "Does 'His Excellency' . . ." Healy and Kutner, p. 203f; O'Toole, p. 364.

Chapter Three

65 "Each cartridge . . ." O'Toole, p. 232.
65 "To fight for my country . . ." Azoy, p. 28.
66 *On to Cuba!* Clifford Westermeier, *Who Rush to Glory,* p. 146.
72 *If anyone thinks . . . ibid.,* p. 241.
75 "All the way . . ." W. B. Gatewood, Jr., *"Smoked Yankees" and the Struggle for Empire,* p. 44.
76 "They fear . . ." *Ibid.,* p. 138f.
78 "His immense abdomen . . ." Friedel, p. 248.

81 "Gentlemen . . ." *Richard Harding Davis, The Cuban and Porto Rican Campaigns,* p. 50.

88 *I heard someone dying* . . . Charles H. Brown, *The Correspondent's War,* pp. 279f.

90 "We should be glad . . ." O'Toole, p. 240f.

Chapter Four

101 "We've got the damn Yankees . . ." Morris, p. 640; "They tried to catch us . . ." Davis, p. 149.

106 "I want ye! . . ." Brown, p. 352.

108 "Now I'm ready . . ." Azoy, pp. 130f; Jack Cameron Dierks, *A Leap to Arms* pp. 103f.

111 "Are you afraid? . . ." Theodore Roosevelt, *The Rough Riders and Men of Action,* p. 82.

112 "No hunting trip . . ." Hugh Thomas, *Cuba,* p. 393; "Well, hell . . ." Davis, p. 224.

116 *The tents* . . . George Kennan, *Campaigning in Cuba,* p. 131f

117 "Cheez . . ." Azoy, p. 124; "Ah, youse can't kill me . . ." Davis, p. 44.

123 "Don't cheer, boys . . ." O'Toole, p. 329.

124 "Oh, captain . . ." Friedel, p. 220; "I do not at all mind . . ." Davis, p. 278.

126 *Snakes* . . . David F. Trask, *The War with Spain in 1898,* p. 327.

Chapter Five

143 "They shall pursue . . ." William T. Sexton, *Soldiers in the Sun: An Adventure in Imperialism,* pp. 75f; "War without quarter . . ." Healy and Kutner, p. 241.

145 "Thicker than buffalo chips . . ." Stuart C. Miller, *"Benevolent Assimilation": The American Conquest of the Philippines, 1899–1903,* p. 76.

147 "Last night . . ." Leon Wolff, *Little Brown Brother: How the United States Purchased and Pacified the Philippines at the Century's Turn,* p. 253; Miller, p. 188.

149 "Then I would treat . . ." Wolff, p. 299; "Why does the American Negro . . ." W. B. Gatewood, Jr., *Black Americans and the White Man's Burden,* p. 285.

151 "we hoped . . ." Richard O'Connor, *Pacific Destiny: An Informal History of the U.S. in the Far East,* p. 283.

153 "Damn 'em . . ." Wolff, p. 236.

158 *My company* . . . Gatewood, *Black Americans,* pp. 277f.

161 "By acknowledging . . ." Wolff, p. 340.

163 "I done my duty . . ." Joseph L. Schlott, *The Ordeal of Samar,* p. 32.

164 "Get your rifles, boys! . . ." *ibid.,* pp. 32f.

165 "Kill and burn . . ." *ibid.,* pp. 71f.

166 "Bloody savages . . ." "loose and violent talk . . ." *ibid.,* pp. 245, 278.

169 "I can never forgive . . ." Miller, p. 272f.

Some More Books

Alden, John. *The American Steel Navy*. Annapolis: U.S. Naval Institute, 1972.

Azoy, A. C. M. *Charge! The Story of the Battle of San Juan Hill*. New York: Longmans, 1961.

Beach, Edward L. *The United States Navy: 200 Years*. New York: Holt, 1986.

Beisner, Robert L. *Twelve Against Empire: The Anti-Imperialists, 1898–1900*. New York: McGraw-Hill, 1968.

Brodie, Bernard. *Sea Power in the Machine Age*. Princeton: Princeton University Press, 1941.

Brown, Charles H. *The Correspondent's War*. New York: Scribner's, 1967.

Coffman, Edward M. *The Old Army: A Portrait of the American Army in Peacetime, 1784–1898*. New York: Oxford University Press, 1986.

Conroy, Robert. *The Battle of Manila Bay: The Spanish-American War in the Philippines.* New York: Macmillan, 1968.
Cosmas, Graham. *An Army for Empire.* Columbia: University of Missouri, 1971.
Davis, Richard Harding. *The Cuban and Porto Rican Campaigns.* Freeport, N.Y.: Books for Libraries. Reprint of a book published in 1898. A classic.
Dierks, Jack Cameron. *A Leap to Arms.* Philadelphia: Lippincott, 1970.
Dunne, Finlay Peter. *Mr. Dooley on Ivrything and Ivrybody.* New York: Dover, 1963.
Foner, Philip S. *The Spanish-Cuban-American War and the Birth of American Imperialism.* 2 vols., New York: Monthly Review Press, 1972.
Freidel, Frank. *The Splendid Little War.* Boston: Little, Brown, 1958.
Funston, Frederick. "The Capture of Emilio Aguinaldo," *Scribner's Magazine* 50 (1911), 522–538.
Gates, John Morgan. *Schoolbooks and Krags: The United States Army in the Philippines, 1898–1902.* Westport, Conn.: Greenwood, 1973.
Gatewood, Willard B., Jr. *"Smoked Yankees" and the Struggle for Empire.* Urbana: University of Illinois Press, 1971.
——. *Black Americans and the White Man's Burden, 1898–1903.* Urbana: University of Illinois Press, 1975.
Graff, Henry F., ed. *American Imperialism and the Philippine Insurrection: Testimony from the Hearings on Affairs in the Philippine Islands before the Senate Committee on the Philippines—1902.* Boston: Little, Brown, 1969.
Healy, Laurin Hall and Luis Kutner. *The Admiral.* New York: Ziff-Davis, 1944. A fine biography of Admiral Dewey.

Hohenberg, John. *Foreign Correspondence: The Great Reporters and Their Times.* New York: Columbia University Press, 1964.

Jones, Virgil C. *Roosevelt's Rough Riders.* Garden City, N.Y.: Doubleday, 1971.

Karnow, Stanley. *In Our Image: America's Empire in the Philippines.* New York: Random House, 1989.

Kennan, George. *Campaigning in Cuba.* New York: The Century Company, 1899.

Linderman, Gerald F. *The Mirror of War: American Society and the Spanish-American War.* Ann Arbor: University of Michigan, 1974.

Miller, Stuart C. *"Benevolent Assimilation": The American Conquest of the Philippines, 1899–1903.* New Haven: Yale University Press, 1982.

Millis, Walter. *The Martial Spirit.* Boston: Houghton, Mifflin, 1931.

Morgan, H. Wayne. *America's Road to Empire: The War with Spain and Overseas Expansion.* New York: Wiley, 1965.

Morris, Edmund. *The Rise of Theodore Roosevelt.* New York: Coward, McCann, 1979.

Morison, Samuel Eliot, Frederick Merk, and Frank Friedel. *Dissent in Three American Wars.* Cambridge, Mass: Harvard University Press, 1970.

O'Connor, Richard. *Pacific Destiny: An Informal History of the U.S. in the Far East.* Boston: Little, Brown, 1969.

O'Toole, G. J. A. *The Spanish War.* New York: W. W. Norton, 1984.

Pratt, Fletcher. *The Navy: A History.* Garden City, N.Y.: Garden City Publishing Co., 1941.

Rickover, H. G. *How the Battleship Maine Was Destroyed.* Washington, D.C.: Government Printing Office, 1976.

Roosevelt, Theodore. *The Rough Riders and Men of Action*. New York: Scribner's, 1926.

Schlott, Joseph L. *The Ordeal of Samar*. Indianapolis: Bobbs-Merrill, 1964.

Sexton, William T. *Soldiers in the Sun: An Adventure in Imperialism*. Harrisburg, Pa.: Military Service Publishing Company, 1939.

Spector, Ronald. *Admiral of the New Empire*. Baton Rouge: Louisiana State University Press, 1974. Another fine biography of Dewey.

Sprout, Harold and Margaret. *The Rise of American Naval Power, 1776–1918*. Princeton: Princeton University Press, 1939.

Stallman, R. W. and E. R. Hagemann, eds. *The War Dispatches of Stephen Crane*. Westport, Conn.: Greenwood Press, 1977.

Sternlicht, Stanford. *McKinley's Bulldog: The Battleship Oregon*. Chicago: Nelson-Hall, 1977.

Swanberg, W. A. *Citizen Hearst*. New York: Scribner's, 1961.

Thomas, Hugh. *Cuba*. London: Eyre and Spottiswoode, 1971.

Trask, David F. *The War with Spain in 1898*. New York: Macmillan, 1981.

Weems, John Edward. *The Fate of the Maine*. New York: Holt, 1958.

Welch, Richard E., Jr. *Response to Imperialism: The United States and the Philippine-American War, 1899–1902*. Chapel Hill: University of North Carolina Press, 1979.

Westermeier, Clifford. *Who Rush to Glory*. Coldwell, Idaho: Caxton Printers, 1958.

Wolff, Leon. *Little Brown Brother: How the United States Purchased and Pacified the Philippines at the Century's Turn*. Garden City, N.Y.: Doubleday, 1961.

Index

176

DATE DUE

SE 26 '91		
OC 17 '91		
OC 24 '91		
OC 31 '91		
FE 9 '9		

973.89
MAR
    Marrin, Albert
        The Spanish-American
        War